WATERSID

nea

Bristol & Bath

Nigel Vile

COUNTRYSIDE BOOKS

NEWBURY, BERKSHIRE

First published 1999
© Nigel Vile 1999
Reprinted 2004

COUNTRYSIDE BOOKS
3 Catherine Road
Newbury, Berkshire

ISBN 1 85306 554 4

Designed by Graham Whiteman
Cover illustration by Colin Doggett
Maps and photographs by the author

Produced through MRM Associates Ltd., Reading
Typeset by Techniset Typesetters, Newton-le-Willows
Printed by Woolnough Bookbinding Ltd., Irthlingborough

Contents

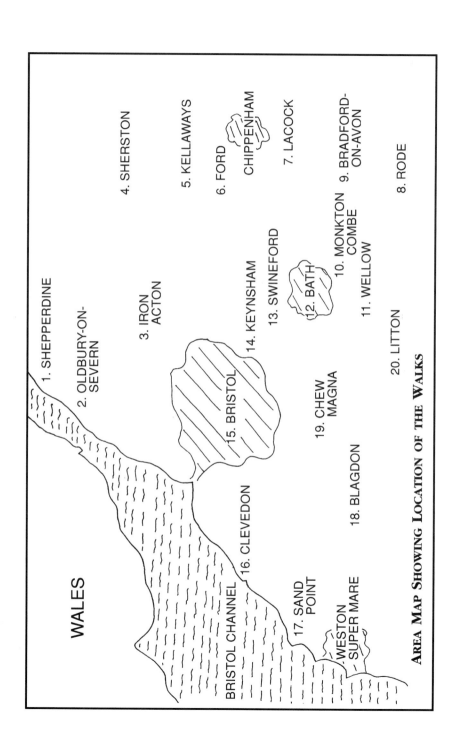

AREA MAP SHOWING LOCATION OF THE WALKS

WALES

BRISTOL CHANNEL

1. SHEPPERDINE
2. OLDBURY-ON-SEVERN
3. IRON ACTON
4. SHERSTON
5. KELLAWAYS
6. FORD
CHIPPENHAM
7. LACOCK
8. RODE
9. BRADFORD-ON-AVON
10. MONKTON COMBE
11. WELLOW
12. BATH
13. SWINEFORD
14. KEYNSHAM
15. BRISTOL
16. CLEVEDON
17. SAND POINT
WESTON SUPER MARE
18. BLAGDON
19. CHEW MAGNA
20. LITTON

numbers have been included should you wish to make precise enquiries about opening times, food availability and so on. Parking at pubs is for patrons only and walkers should always ask the landlord's permission before leaving their car in the pub car park while they are actually walking. And on the subject of parking: if you find space in a village street please make sure that you are not blocking any entrances or exits.

All of the usual advice should go without saying. The British climate almost demands that walkers carry waterproofs, whilst the proximity of water necessarily means mud. Suitable footwear is therefore essential – and don't forget to remove muddy boots before going into a pub. Adhering to these sensible demands will mean that you gain the maximum enjoyment from this book. I wish you many hours of happy waterside walking.

Nigel Vile

THE RIVER SEVERN AT SHEPPERDINE

A series of quiet byways and lanes wend their way across the Severn Vale to the river's shoreline at Shepperdine. The Severn here is over one mile wide, and the views across the water towards the Forest of Dean are quite exceptional. The true grandeur of one of Britain's great rivers will be a lasting memory from this waterside walk.

The river Severn

Below the Cotswold Hills lies the Severn Vale, contrasting landscapes as different as the proverbial 'chalk and cheese'. The Vale is a secluded backwater of country lanes and traditional farmhouses, surrounded by diminutive orchards and rich grazing land. It is a landscape that has escaped the worst excesses of modern arable farming, a reminder of the agricultural landscape of a bygone era.

At Shepperdine, in the heart of the Vale, the river Severn has almost completed its 210-mile long journey from an upland peat bog below Plynlimon in mid-Wales to the sea. The river is by now tidal, and at low tide the mud flats attract a wide variety of waders, with dunlin, curlew and redshank being the most numerous species.

The Severn hereabouts is also navigable, with the occasional sea-going vessel plying its way upstream to the inland dock complex at Sharpness. The pitfalls of navigation along this treacherous tidal estuary are lessened by a contrasting pair of lighthouses that guide ships up the river. Alongside a traditional wooden light tower stands a functional modern beacon, both serving to direct vessels through the deep-water channel that cuts its way through the river's mud banks.

Boats have been navigating their way up the river for hundreds of years, and in years gone by Severn barges laden with Forest of Dean coal would wend their way downstream. On the river bank at Shepperdine was this isolated hostelry – the New Inn – where the bargees would rest awhile for the occasional pint ... or six! On those occasions when they were simply too inebriated to risk their vessels on the river, the excuse to their masters for late sailings was that their vessels had become 'windbound'. The name stuck, and what was originally a nickname is today the name of an inn that lies at the end of a cul-de-sac lane below the Severn's sea defences. It has even been known for floodwater to pour down the inn's chimneys during severe storms.

Internally, the Windbound conveys the atmosphere of this most romantic of locations. Prints and watercolours of local scenes adorn the walls, whilst local salmon putchers are also displayed around the bar. These conical-shaped baskets would face upstream to capture the local salmon on the ebb tide as they migrated through the estuary.

As well as a warm welcome from its open fires on cold days, the Windbound offers welcome sustenance to those intrepid visitors who manage to seek out its isolated location. Regular bar food includes soup, sandwiches, ploughman's and salads, with a good selection of daily specials available that could include sausage casserole, tuna and pasta bake or Spanish tortilla. Bass, Tetley Bitter and Flowers Original are amongst the beers available at this fine riverside inn.

Telephone: 01454 414343.

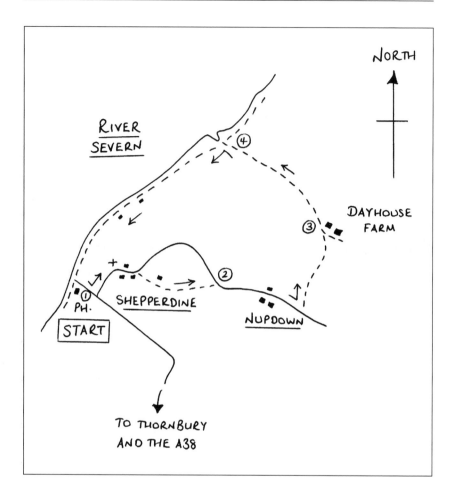

- **HOW TO GET THERE:** Follow the A38 northwards out of Bristol for 14 miles until you see 'Oldbury-on-Severn' signposted on the left-hand side. As you approach Oldbury, Shepperdine appears on the signposts. Follow these signs for Shepperdine – which soon include the Windbound. At the end of a cul-de-sac just below the Severn lies the Windbound Inn.
- **PARKING:** There is a large car park outside the Windbound Inn, just below the Severn's flood defences.
- **LENGTH OF THE WALK:** 4 miles. Maps: OS Landranger 162 Gloucester and the Forest of Dean or OS Outdoor Leisure 14 Wye Valley (GR 613961).

The pub at Shepperdine

THE WALK

1. Walk inland from the Windbound Inn for 200 yards to a road junction, and turn left along the lane signposted to Hill and Rockhampton. Follow this lane for 600 yards, passing Shepperdine's diminutive wooden church alongside Manor Farm, before reaching Shepperdine Farm. Just past Shepperdine Farm, turn right along a signposted footpath. This is initially a gravelled drive leading to an isolated property called The Laurels. Continue along what becomes a grassy track that passes in front of The Laurels. Almost straightaway, this track bears left alongside the far side of the property. Instead of bearing left along this track, pass through the gateway directly ahead, cross the field to a gap in the hedge opposite and, in the next field, follow the watercourse on the left around to a gateway in the left-hand corner of the field. Head directly across the next field to a gate on the far side, where the fieldpath rejoins the lane leading to Hill.

2. Turn right, and follow this lane for ¼ mile to the hamlet of Nupdown, deep in the Severn Vale. About 100 yards beyond Nupdown Farm, follow the signposted footpath on the left-hand side. Keep on this path as it crosses two fields to reach Dayhouse Farm, walking alongside a stream on the right. At the far side of the second field, alongside the farm complex, turn left for a few yards before crossing a footbridge on the right to follow a path into a collection of farm buildings. Once across this bridge, turn left alongside a barn before entering an open field.

3. Walk to the far end of this field, pass through a gateway and walk the length of the next field, heading towards the Severn. At the far end of this field, pass through another gateway and continue along the length of one final field down to the river.

4. Climb up onto the raised embankment that acts as a flood defence, and follow the river to the left for $1\frac{1}{4}$ miles back to the Windbound Inn. The views are quite exceptional – upstream to Sharpness, across the Severn to the Forest of Dean and downstream towards the first and second Severn crossings. Along the way, the path passes that pair of lighthouses that guide vessels up the treacherous estuary towards the docks at Sharpness. On reaching the inn, a left turn will return you to the car park.

Places Of Interest Nearby

Just north-east of Shepperdine lies the small town of Berkeley, where visitors can spend a pleasant few hours visiting the *Edward Jenner Museum* as well as *Berkeley Castle*. The castle contains the cell where Edward II was murdered in 1327, apparently by a red-hot iron being thrust into his bowels! For further details, telephone the nearest Tourist Information Centre on 01453 765768.

THE RIVER SEVERN AT OLDBURY

Enjoy a gentle stroll along flat paths that border the river Severn. The only climb, a very modest ascent, is to reach St Arilda's church at Oldbury, from where fine views of the locality can be had from the comfort of a churchyard seat!

Oldbury Pill

Although some distance from the river, Oldbury would literally have been 'on-Severn' in centuries past, when floods frequently swamped the local low-lying land. To the south of the village, safe from floodwater on a small hill or knoll, lies St Arilda's church overlooking the mighty Severn. Downstream lie the Severn Bridges, and upstream the towers of Oldbury Power Station. Across the river lie Chepstow, the Forest of Dean and the foothills of the Welsh mountains.

The river Severn rises on the eastern slopes of Plynlimon, deep in mid-Wales, from where its 210 mile journey to the Bristol Channel commences. At Oldbury, the river used to be worked by local fishermen using racks of conical-shaped baskets or 'putchers' to capture Severn salmon. The open ends of these putchers faced upstream to capture the salmon on the ebb tide as they migrated through the estuary. This fishing technique – still practised further afield along the riverbank – is unique to the Severn.

The estuary supports large numbers of birds which have adapted to feed on the abundant supply of small, mud-dwelling creatures. Waders, such as the dunlin, are especially common during the winter months. Lists of species to spot would be futile, with so much depending upon the tides and the seasons, so come armed with your binoculars and bird-spotting books.

Having enjoyed a waterside walk by the Severn, you come to the appropriately named Anchor Inn at journey's end. Here there is evidence of salmon fishing on the river, with illustrations of the putchers on a rather impressive inn sign. Perhaps of even more interest is one of the floral displays outside the inn, where a putcher has been converted into a rather unusual hanging basket.

The Anchor, with its beams and stonework, oak tables and cushioned window seats, exudes a most traditional feel. The inn's ever changing menu attracts visitors from far and wide. Examples of dishes are leek and potato bake, seafood pancake, Painswick pork and a wide selection of steaks. The puddings are equally enticing.

A good range of real ales is also available at the Anchor, with Bass, Butcombe Best Bitter and Theakston Old Peculier being particularly popular choices. With a number of good quality wines, over 75 malts and Inch's cider, just about every conceivable taste should be catered for at this fine hostelry deep in the Severn Vale. Telephone: 01454 413331.

- **HOW TO GET THERE:** Take the B4061 road through Thornbury and, on the northern outskirts of the town, a minor road on the left is signposted to Oldbury-on-Severn. In the village, turn left at the crossroads and the Anchor Inn soon appears on the left-hand side of the road.
- **PARKING:** There is a car park for patrons alongside the inn. There is also room for roadside parking opposite the hostelry.
- **LENGTH OF THE WALK:** 2 miles. Maps: OS Landrangers 162 Gloucester and the Forest of Dean or 172 Bristol and Bath or OS Explorer 167 Thornbury (GR 608923).

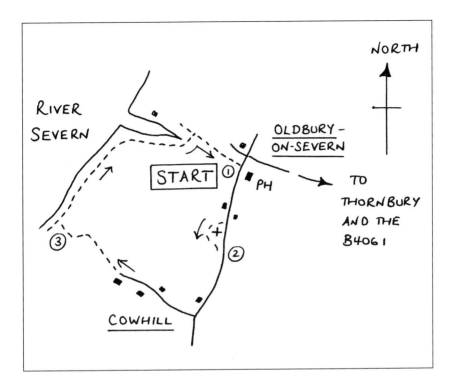

THE WALK

1. Follow the lane to the south out of the village, climbing the hill past the village school to reach St Arilda's church. Turn right, and follow the path into the churchyard to enjoy the fine views across the Severn Estuary. Continue along the path around to the back of the church, before following some steps downhill to a metal kissing gate, beyond which the path rejoins the lane.

2. Continue along the lane for 300 yards until, a short distance past a detached house called Church View, the walk turns right along a cul-de-sac lane. Follow this lane through the hamlet of Cowhill, passing cottages and Manor Farm, until the metalled lane ends at Cowhill Farm. Continue following what becomes an unmetalled track beyond the farm for 300 yards until, after bearing left and right in quick succession, the track reaches a gateway and an open field.

3. Cross this field to its far right-hand corner, cross a gate and climb

St Arilda's church

the flood defences to reach the banks of the Severn. Follow these defences upstream for ³/₄ mile in the direction of Oldbury Power Station. Continue along the raised embankment as it bears right alongside Oldbury Pill, now home to the local yacht club. Cross a sluice gate at the eastern end of Oldbury Pill, before turning right to follow the yacht club access lane back into Oldbury-on-Severn. The access lane joins the road opposite the Anchor Inn.

PLACES OF INTEREST NEARBY

At the nearby *Oldbury Nuclear Power Station,* a visitors centre explains the role of nuclear power in contemporary Britain. Visitors can also discover what actually goes on in those vast concrete generators dotted around Britain's coastline. Telephone Oldbury Power Station on 01454 416631 for details.

THE RIVER FROME NEAR IRON ACTON

Discover a rural oasis in a landscape that is rapidly being eroded by modern development. Riverside paths, green lanes and waterside meadows provide a much needed buffer between Bristol's north-eastern suburbs and the ever expanding new town of Yate. The walk explores the countryside south-west of Iron Acton, and most of the return leg is alongside the Bristol Frome.

The river Frome

The Bristol Frome rises in Dodington Park on the Cotswold escarpment, before flowing in a south-westerly direction for 20 miles to join the Avon in the centre of Bristol. The name 'Frome' is derived from the Anglo-Saxon 'frum', which translates as 'rapid' or 'vigorous'. The river's power was put to good use very early on, with as many as eight mills operating along the Frome between

17

Frenchay and Iron Acton. This walk follows a section of what has been designated as the 'Frome Valley Walkway', a series of footpaths and permissive rights of way that enable the river to be followed from its source in the Southwolds into the heart of Bristol.

The walk begins in Iron Acton, which translates literally as 'the oak settlement with iron'. This linear village was the home of the Poyntz family for many centuries, with the ornate cross in the churchyard thought to be a memorial to one of the family members. Iron Acton Court, the family home, built in the 16th century, lies to the north of the village.

Hover's Lane, a green track, is followed across the fields to neighbouring Frampton Cotterell. Although St Peter's church in Frampton was largely rebuilt in the 19th century, there are relics from an earlier era including a 17th-century brass to John Symes and a chained copy of Bishop Jewel's *Apology for the Church of England*, dated 1568. From St Peter's, the walk follows the Frome Valley Walkway back to Iron Acton, passing Algars Manor and Chill Wood along the way. The original manor was Tudor, but it was largely rebuilt in the 18th century. Alongside the manor lies a picturesque grist mill, first mentioned in the Domesday Book of 1086. Chill Wood is a delightful deciduous woodland just upstream of the manor. It marks the site of coal mining back in the 17th century, although today's visitors will be more impressed with the wood's carpet of flowers in springtime.

Back in Iron Acton at journey's end lies the White Hart. Attached to the wall of the inn is one of those yellow and black AA signs, informing visitors that the White Hart lies exactly 112 miles from London. This timeless feel continues inside the inn, where black beams, wood panelling and lanterns give a most traditional atmosphere.

The White Hart is now part of the national chain of 'Hungry House Bars and Grills'. The menu on offer reflects this chain's emphasis, with various steak dishes, lamb, roast chicken, curries and lasagne. Fish dishes include cod and plaice, with the fisherman's pie proving a tempting option. Perhaps the greatest challenge would be the dish advertised as a pound of sausages with onion gravy! This is certainly designed to restore those calories lost along the way on this riverside ramble in the Frome Valley. Beers available include Courage Bitter and Directors, plus John Smith's.

Telephone: 01454 228228.

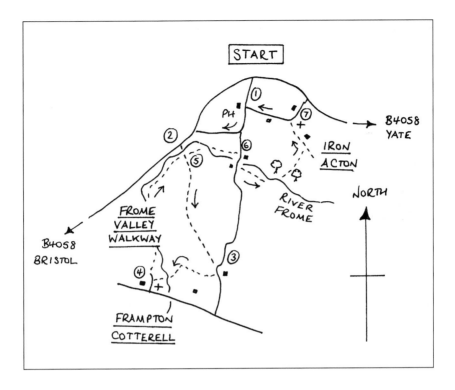

- **HOW TO GET THERE:** Iron Acton lies just off the B4058 Bristol to Yate road, 1¹/₂ miles from Yate. The main road effectively bypasses the village, which is clearly signposted.
- **PARKING:** Park at the western end of the village High Street, in the proximity of the White Hart Inn.
- **LENGTH OF THE WALK:** 4¹/₂ miles. Maps: OS Landranger 172 Bristol and Bath or OS Explorer 167 Thornbury (GR 677836).

THE WALK

1. Walk to the end of Iron Acton's High Street and turn left in front of the White Hart Inn. Follow the road out of the village for just under ¹/₂ mile to reach the busy B4058, keeping right at one junction along the way as well as crossing the railway line to Thornbury. Turn left at the main road, following the path that cuts a course through the grass verge alongside it. Continue for 200 yards.

2. Turn left by the entrance to Iron Acton Stables to follow a track

19

The pub at the start of the walk

signposted to Frampton End. This track – shown on the Pathfinder sheet as Hover's Lane – crosses the Frome very early on before winding its way across country to join Frampton End Road.

3. Turn right and, in just 50 yards, cross a stone slab stile on the right to follow a fieldpath signposted to St Peter's church in Frampton. Head directly across the first field to a stile in the opposite hedgerow and, in the next field, continue in the same direction to a stile alongside a prominent oak tree. In a third field, cross to the trees opposite and follow the woodland to the right around to a stile in the corner of the field. Cross this stile and follow the path to the left – this is the trackbed of a former mineral line that ran to an iron mine in Frampton. In 100 yards, the path drops down the embankment on the right to a stile and an open field. Cross to the far left-hand corner of this field, pass through a gateway and follow the drive up to Mill Lane in Frampton.

4. A detour to the left brings you to St Peter's church – we turn right to follow the signposted Frome Valley Walkway. Continue along the lane to a works yard, walk past the various workshops and bear right to a stile in the corner of the complex, just past the last shed on the right. Once across this stile, the path joins the banks of the Frome. Follow the right edge of the first field by the river to a stile. In the next field, literally join the river bank and follow the well-worn path beside the water upstream for 600 yards until you reach a metal footbridge. Cross the river, turn left and continue following the river upstream across an arable field.

At the far side of the field, follow the path through a small area of overgrown scrubland to a stile and a paddock. Cross this field to a stile in the left-hand corner behind a green shed. Go over the next small paddock to a stile in the corner before crossing yet another field to a stile in its left-hand corner. All the while, the Frome is flowing along behind the trees and bushes on the left. Once across that last stile, you will find yourself on that track by Iron Acton Stables which was followed at the outset.

5. Cross the track and the stile opposite into a field to continue following the Frome Valley Walkway upstream. In the far left corner of this field, cross a stile and follow a path through an area of scrub by the Frome to a stile and a flight of steps leading up to a bridge across the Frome. This is once again the remains of that mineral line passed earlier near Frampton. Cross the river and a stile on the right, before following the river upstream. Where the lawn ends, cross a stile and continue along the Frome Valley Walkway as it bears left away from the river uphill to a stile in the corner of the field and Frampton End Road.

6. Turn right, follow the lane down past Algars Manor, cross the Frome and turn left, continuing to follow the river upstream. In $1/4$ mile, cross the river via a sluice and follow the path into Chill Wood. Pass through the woodland to a gateway and a field, clip the corner of the field and follow a flight of steps on the left up onto the railway line to Thornbury. Cross the tracks, and descend the far side of the embankment into a field. Head uphill to the top left corner of this field, cross a stone slab stile and follow an enclosed path behind some houses to Iron Acton church. Continue along the path to the left of the church to reach the High Street, and turn left.

7. Walk the length of this attractive village street back to the White Hart Inn.

SHERSTON AND THE SOURCE
OF THE AVON

Residents of Bath and Bristol will know that the Avon flows down from Chippenham and Bradford to their cities, but what happens further upstream? Discover the source of this great river just a mile-or-two upstream of the old market centre of Sherston, now a sizeable Cotswolds village.

The infant river Avon

In many ways, it could be misleading to describe this as a waterside walk. As the Avon is followed upstream from Malmesbury, it soon alters its shape and form from that of a river to a diminutive stream that in high summer often resembles little more than a ditch. Discovering the source of a river, however, is a fascinating pastime, especially a river that is dear to the hearts of both Bathonians and Bristolians.

The source of the Avon is open to some debate. The Ordnance Survey map show two tributaries above Malmesbury – the Tetbury Branch and the Sherston Branch. Follow the Sherston Branch upstream, and you will arrive at Joyce's Pool on the edge of Didmarton. A plaque beside the pool records this spot as being the source of the river Avon. In dry weather, however, such claims appear rather spurious with the watercourses south of Joyce's Pool resembling dry ditches.

A more permanent source to the river is found a mile south at Crow Down Springs, where a diminutive stream flows through a secluded valley. The scene is seemingly a million miles away from that grand river that passes through the heart of Bath and Bristol.

Away from these watery origins, this walk explores the Cotswold villages of Didmarton, Sopworth and Sherston. Sopworth, with its farms, church and manor house, is a particularly attractive settlement. Brian Woodruffe, in his book *Wiltshire Villages*, includes Sopworth amongst his favourite 20 villages in the county – praise indeed in a county that has so many attractive villages.

Sherston is an altogether more substantial settlement. It acquired borough status in the 15th century, and boasts many fine houses that span a period of some 500 years along its High Street. At the top end of the village stands Holy Cross church, with a figure of the mysterious Rattlebone on the exterior wall of the porch. Local legend maintains that Rattlebone had his finest hour when fighting for Edmund Ironside against the Danes in 1016 when 'the great Sherston champion, severely wounded in the fight, heroically applied a tile-stone to his stomach to prevent his bowels gushing out'.

The Rattlebone Inn is a handsome 16th-century Cotswold-stone pub that stands opposite Holy Cross church. With its various nooks and crannies, pink walls and beams, pews and settles, it exudes an atmosphere of centuries past.

In addition to filled rolls, ploughman's and soup, the Rattlebone Inn offers a range of well-prepared dishes to its visitors. These include such old favourites as breaded plaice and steak and kidney pie, as well as selections such as chilli with tortilla chips, smoked salmon and yoghurt mousse and vegetable crêpes. If the calorie count permits, a dessert such as fruit crumble or treacle pie will soon restore any energy lost on this walk of discovery.

As for drinks, a pint of Smiles Best, Smiles Golden or that old standby Bass is particularly recommended, any of which will

23

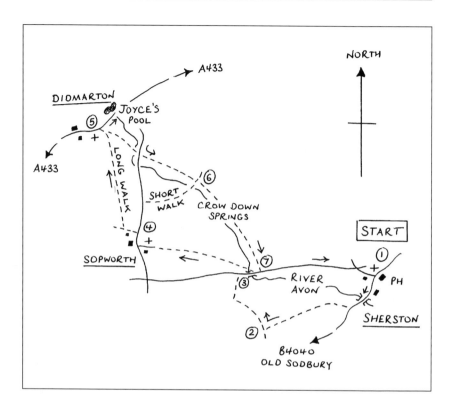

certainly quench thirsts brought about by this lengthy stroll to the source of the Avon. If the weather allows, food and drink can be enjoyed in the Rattlebone's small garden.

Telephone: 01666 840871.

- **HOW TO GET THERE:** The Rattlebone Inn lies at the northern end of Sherston's High Street, opposite the village church. Sherston lies 6 miles west of Malmesbury on the B4040 Old Sodbury road.
- **PARKING:** There is a small car park alongside the Rattlebone for patrons. A better alternative is to park in Sherston's wide High Street, which is literally next door to the inn.
- **LENGTH OF THE WALK:** 4½ or 7 miles, with the longer walk including both Crow Down Springs and Joyce's Pool. Maps: OS Landranger 173 Swindon and Devizes or OS Explorer 168 Stroud & Malmesbury (GR 854860).

THE WALK

1. Walk the length of Sherston's High Street, and follow the B4040 downhill and out of the village, crossing the river Avon along the way. Immediately past the last cottage on the right as you leave the village, cross a gate into a field to follow a poorly signposted footpath. Climb the steep bank immediately ahead to reach a wall at the top of the field. Follow this wall to the right and on around to the far left-hand corner of the field. Pass through a gateway, before following the left edge of the next field to a gate in the far left-hand corner. Head directly across the middle of the next field to a gate on the far side.

2. Beyond this gateway, you join Shallowbrooks Lane. Follow this track to the right for ¹/₂ mile until you reach the Sherston to Sopworth road, keeping right at a junction along the way where the left turn is a driveway leading to Sandy Farm. Turn right on reaching the road, and in 150 yards you will cross the river Avon at Stan Bridge.

3. Immediately past the bridge, turn left through a gateway to follow a signposted footpath into a field. Head across to the diminutive footbridge across the infant river Avon, and continue to a gateway in the far right corner of the field. Follow the right edge of the next field to a gate in the corner and, in the next field, follow the left edge to the far corner. At the far side of the field, 15 yards down from the left-hand corner, cross a stile into a small paddock. Follow the left edge of this paddock to a stile and a path running alongside Sopworth church.

Pass through the churchyard, and follow the lane ahead past School House and out onto the main road in Sopworth. Turn right and continue for about 100 yards.

4. For the shorter walk, continue along the main road for a further 400 yards, turn right along a track and in ¹/₂ mile rejoin the walk at point 6 below, turning right just beyond the river Avon.

For the longer walk, turn left immediately past Wiltshire Path Cottage, onto a signposted bridleway. Just a few yards along this bridleway, follow a signposted path on the right past a handgate and stile and on along the right edge of a small plantation to a second stile. Follow the fence on the right in the next field for just a few

25

yards to another stile and open fields. Cross this stile, and bear half left across the bottom corner of a field to a stone slab stile halfway along the left-hand field boundary. Go over this stile, turn right and follow the wall on the right to a stile in the top corner of the field. Hidden in the undulating countryside on the right is the infant river Avon. Cross the next field, walking in the same direction, to a stile at the bottom of the field. Follow the right edge of the next field to a gate in the right-hand corner. Pass through this gateway, and immediately pass through another gateway on the left. Head directly up the next field towards Didmarton to a gate in the top left corner, by a small stable block. Follow the track beyond this gateway down to the main A433.

5. On the left is St Lawrence's church, well worth a detour to discover its triple-decked pulpit and high-backed wooden pews. To continue the walk, cross the main road, and follow the pavement opposite to the right for 100 yards to reach Joyce's Pool, one of the sources of the river Avon. Continue along the main road for 50 yards, before turning right along an unsignposted lane. In 600 yards, having passed a sewage works on the right and a bridlepath on the left, a signed footpath crosses the lane. Cross the stile on the left, and head across to the far side of the field. About 20 yards down from the far left corner, cross a stone slab stile. In the next field, make for a gate almost in the bottom right corner where you meet and cross a track leading to Field Barn. (This is the track that the shorter walk followed from the Sopworth road.)

6. Follow the signposted footpath into open fields. Continue along the right edge of the next four fields, all the while keeping just above the infant river Avon which lies down in the meadows on the right. Pass through a gateway at the end of the fourth field, before crossing a fifth field to an electricity sub-station in the left-hand corner. Just below this sub-station, join the Sopworth to Sherston road.

7. Turn left, and follow the lane for $^3/_4$ mile back into Sherston. At the crossroads on the edge of the village, turn right along Court Road which returns you to Sherston's High Street.

THE RIVER AVON AT KELLAWAYS

Enjoy a gentle walk along the banks of the river Avon, set in a landscape that once inspired the Victorian cleric Francis Kilvert. Along the way, discover a spectacular raised causeway that was built to keep the feet of travellers dry whilst crossing the river's floodplain.

Maud Heath's Causeway

In its upper reaches between the hilltop town of Malmesbury and Chippenham, the river Avon crosses an area of flat, low-lying agricultural land that has always been prone to flooding. In the 15th century, a Chippenham market trader by the name of Maud Heath, incensed at the prospect of wet feet on her weekly tramp to market, bequeathed a sum of money for the construction of a causeway across the floodplain.

Maud Heath's Causeway, 4½ miles long, is at road level for much of its length, although at Kellaways there is an altogether more dramatic construction. There 60 raised arches, 6 feet above road

27

level, carry the causeway over the Avon and its immediate meadowland. A monument at the western end of this raised causeway pays tribute to Maud Heath.

Kellaways lies just east of Langley Burrell, Maud Heath's birthplace, a village also associated with Francis Kilvert. This Victorian cleric was born at nearby Hardenhuish, and was curate in Langley Burrell between 1863 and 1864. The church lies a little way off the walk – ½ mile north on the B4069 in the grounds of Langley House – but a detour by car at the end of this ramble is worthwhile.

Kilvert loved the great outdoors, and wrote most descriptively of his passion for walking out along country byways. Walking along the banks of the Avon below Kellaways, being disturbed by little else than the flapping of a nervous heron's wings, it is not difficult to feel a little of the spirit that so inspired Francis Kilvert.

A different kind of spirit is served at the Brewery Arms in Langley Burrell, a whitewashed cottage-style hostelry named after the brewery that once operated in the neighbouring building. Sadly, the brewery is no more, the former brewhouse now serving as the regional headquarters of the National Farmers Union. The Brewery Arms has public and lounge bars, which connect with a dining room at the rear of the inn. Wooden settles, thick beams and an open fireplace give the inn a most traditional feel, with prints and displays of plates completing the decor.

In addition to such pub staples as jacket potatoes, sandwiches and ploughman's, the Brewery Arms offers customers an à la carte menu as well as a range of daily specials. The specials are generous and well-prepared, and have included pheasant in a red wine sauce, liver and pork paté and home-made leek and potato soup. Being located in Wiltshire, a pint of locally brewed beer is almost obligatory. Perhaps Wadworth 6X from Devizes or Ushers Best Bitter from Trowbridge should be the order of the day.

Telephone: 01249 652707.

- **HOW TO GET THERE:** Follow the B4069 Lyneham road out of Chippenham for 1 mile before turning right along an unclassified road signposted to East Tytherton. Follow this road through Langley Burrell and, in another ¾ mile, you will reach the raised section of Maud Heath's Causeway at Kellaways.

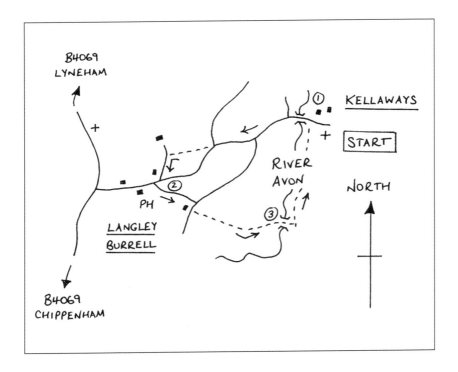

- **PARKING:** There is room for roadside parking at either end of the causeway.
- **LENGTH OF THE WALK:** 2½ miles. Maps: OS Landranger 173 Swindon and Devizes or OS Explorer 156 Chippenham (GR 947758).

THE WALK

1. Follow Maud Heath's Causeway back towards Langley Burrell for ½ mile, passing under the main South Wales railway line along the way. The causeway is little more than a pavement for most of this section of the walk. At a road junction, left to Langley Burrell, right to Sutton Benger, continue directly ahead across a small area of scrubland to a stile and an arable field. Cross to the far left-hand corner of this field – following the field boundary to the left if crops are growing – where you reach a lane leading to Manor Farm. Turn left along this lane, which joins the main street in Langley Burrell in 300 yards.

2. Turn right and, in just a few yards, left along Crossing Lane. The

29

The Brewery Arms, Langley Burrell

Brewery Arms, incidentally, is located just 50 yards along the road from Crossing Lane. Continue along Crossing Lane to a humped-back bridge across the railway line. Cross the railway, and continue along a lane for 100 yards to a road junction. Turn right and, in 75 yards, turn left along a signposted bridlepath just past Dolphin Cottage. Follow this path along the right edge of a field towards the far corner.

In the far corner of the field, there is a footbridge across a stream on the right. Ignore this bridge, continuing instead along the bottom end of the field for some 20 yards to a gateway and a second footbridge on the right. Cross this footbridge, and turn left in the adjoining field to follow a man-made channel on the left-hand side. Follow this channel to the far corner of the field to reach a footbridge across the river Avon.

3. Cross the river, and turn left to follow the Avon upstream for $^3/_4$ mile to the raised causeway. In the top corner of the field immediately before the road, a flight of steps returns the walk to the raised section of Maud Heath's Causeway.

THE BY BROOK NEAR FORD

The By Brook, a clear trout stream, meanders through some delightful scenery within easy reach of Bath and Bristol. Enjoy a pleasant hour or two exploring this most picturesque of the Bristol Avon's tributaries.

The By Brook

The By Brook is perhaps the most attractive tributary of the river Avon. Rising deep in the Southern Cotswolds near Tormarton, it carves a course through narrow flat-bottomed valleys before joining the Avon at Bathford. Along the way, its waters add beauty and delight to the villages of Castle Combe, Ford, Slaughterford and Box. This short walk explores a delightful stretch of the By Brook between Ford and Slaughterford. At Slaughterford, the river has been harnessed over the years to power local mills. The derelict waterwheel of a former rag mill is passed in the village, as is St Nicholas' church, standing in splendid isolation in a field.

St Nicholas' lay in ruinous decay for 200 years, having been ransacked by Cromwell's men, but was rebuilt and reopened in 1823. One local guidebook declares it to be 'so devoid of interest as to be worth a visit' – somewhat harsh criticism! The riverside path between the two villages runs through a well-wooded valley. Wildlife abounds, with buzzards, dippers, kingfishers and herons being just some of the birds to keep an eye out for. Fish-spotting is another possibility, with the By Brook being a noted trout fishery.

The walk starts and ends at Ford, a traditional stop on the old coach road from London to Bristol. The local inn, the White Hart, has never ceased to be an attraction for travellers from London. Internally, there are heavy black beams, tub armchairs, polished wooden tables, advertising mirrors and a fireplace dated 1553. In the spring and summer, however, you will inevitably prefer to enjoy your food and drink on the inn's terrace overlooking the By Brook. The food selections change from week to week but have included broccoli and blue cheese crumble, beef stroganoff, wild boar sausages with mustard and tarragon sauce and roast pork tenderloin with caramelised apples, marinaded sultanas and a cider sauce. Lesser appetites might opt for ploughman's, sandwiches or home-made soup.

Lovers of fine beer and cider are really spoiled for choice at the White Hart. In addition to farm ciders, excellent real ales including Badger Tanglefoot, Hook Norton, Shepherd Neame Spitfire and Fuller's London Pride are normally available for customers. Don't forget the drive home before embarking on a miniature beer festival, however! This remote hostelry no longer lies on one of the traditional coaching routes, and a car is almost obligatory. Telephone: 01249 782213.

- **HOW TO GET THERE:** Ford lies on the A420 between Chippenham and Bristol. The White Hart Inn lies just south of the main road, on the lane signposted to Colerne.
- **PARKING:** There are car parks for patrons behind the White Hart Inn. There is also a layby back on the main A420 opposite Ford church. The walk is described from the layby, although the route passes the White Hart very early on.
- **LENGTH OF THE WALK:** 2 miles. Maps: OS Landranger 173 Swindon and Devizes or OS Explorer 156 Chippenham (GR 842749).

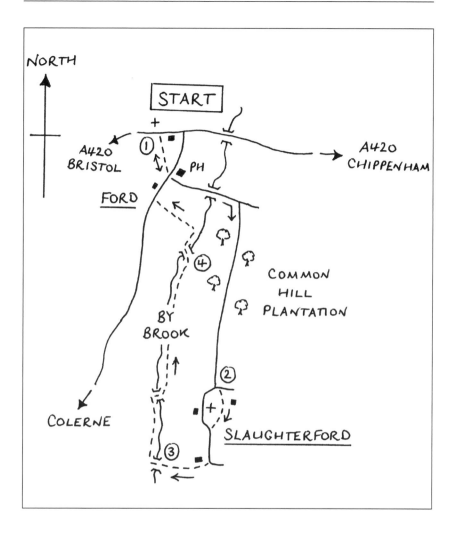

THE WALK

1. At the western end of the layby, follow the steps and the path on the left down to the White Hart Inn. Cross the road, and follow the lane alongside the pub and across the By Brook. Just past the river, turn right along a quiet lane that climbs through Common Hill Plantation to reach a junction on the edge of Slaughterford in $1/2$ mile.

2. Cross the stile opposite, and follow a fieldpath to the left of St

33

The derelict waterwheel at Slaughterford

Nicholas' church and down to a metal gate. Continue along the raised path beside the road through Slaughterford. In 150 yards, on a left-hand bend, turn right along a footpath that shortly passes a ruinous mill and waterwheel on the right.

3. Just past this old mill, cross the By Brook using a wooden footbridge. Continue ahead following the riverside path upstream to the next bridge alongside a sluice. Cross the river and turn left, following the By Brook upstream through three fields. Pass through a gap in the hedge at the far side of the first field, and cross a stile at the far side of the second field.

4. At the far side of the third field, cross the By Brook using a footbridge by a seat. Continue upstream alongside the river past two further seats before bearing left away from the By Brook to a gate and the Colerne to Ford road. Turn right and, shortly, you will return to the White Hart Inn. Retrace your steps up the footpath back to the layby.

THE RIVER AVON AT LACOCK

A quiet stroll along the river to neighbouring Reybridge will form a pleasant contrast to the time you will inevitably spend exploring Lacock and its distinguished abbey. The walk is set deep in the Wiltshire countryside, with the Avon meandering across its floodplain beneath the wooded slopes of Bowden Hill and Naish Hill.

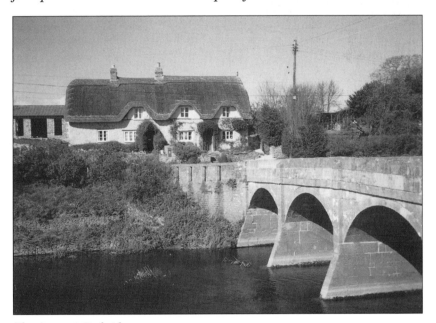

The Avon at Reybridge

Between Lacock and Reybridge, the Bristol Avon winds its way across a flat clay vale that, even in these days of flood relief schemes and sluice gates, is still prone to flooding. At Lacock, one of two bridges across the river stands on dry land awaiting floodwater, whilst in both villages pedestrians find the walkway elevated onto a raised causeway to keep feet dry following heavy rainfall.

The river bank walk between Lacock and Reybridge is a delightful rural haven. Set against a backdrop of Bowden Hill and Naish Hill, an assortment of flora and fauna have their habitat along this section of the river. It should not be difficult in the summer months to spot dragonflies, waterlilies, teazles and moorhen along the course of the river, with timid rabbits feeding alongside in the riverside meadows.

Back in Lacock, the visitor will discover a village described as 'easily the most beautiful in Wiltshire'. Centred upon four streets – Church Street, West and East Streets and the High Street – the overall effect is very much that of a medieval town. There are attractive houses covering every century from the 13th to the 18th, as well as Lacock Abbey, the Fox Talbot Museum of Photography, St Cyriac's church, a fine tithe barn, the village cross and a handsome packhorse bridge across Bide Brook, a tributary of the Avon. The whole is admirably overseen and managed by the National Trust, with even the telephone box being an unobtrusive shade of grey!

At the eastern end of the High Street lies the Red Lion Inn. This tall, red-brick hostelry is faced with golden limestone, a sure sign that geologically Lacock is at the divide between the clay vale of Wiltshire and the Cotswold stone country further west. The Red Lion exudes a delightful rural charm, with yokes, cart-shafts and assorted agricultural memorabilia dividing the bar area into a number of smaller, more intimate areas. With its flagstone flooring, open log fire in winter, displays of stuffed birds and animals, plates and paintings, this fine Georgian inn will provide welcome sustenance after a riverside walk to Reybridge.

In addition to such staple bar food as soup, sandwiches and ploughman's, the Red Lion's menu also includes scampi, salmon steaks with white wine and cream sauce and rump steaks. This is a Wadworth inn, a local brewery based in Devizes that is best known for its 6X brew. Lesser known Wadworth brews available at the Red Lion include Henry's IPA and Farmer's Glory, neither of which will disappoint lovers of real ale.

Telephone: 01249 730456.

- **HOW TO GET THERE:** Lacock lies just off the A350 midway between Chippenham and Melksham. Follow the signs to the visitors' car park, which is located just to the east of the village High Street.
- **PARKING:** A free visitors' car park in Lacock is signposted from the A350.
- **LENGTH OF THE WALK:** 2½ miles. Maps: OS Landranger 173 Swindon and Devizes or OS Explorer 156 Chippenham (GR 918683).

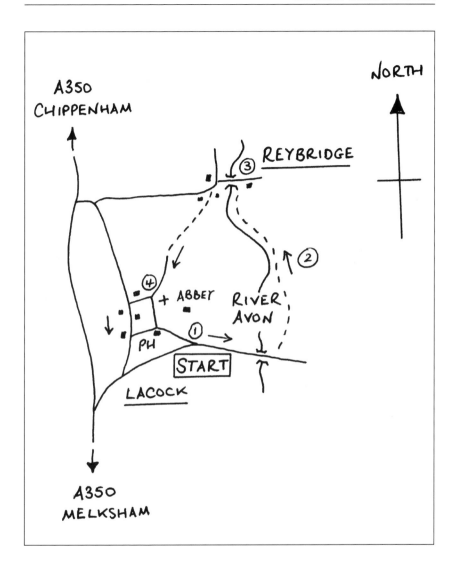

THE WALK

1. Leave the car park and follow the road to the right as it heads out of Lacock. Across the fields on the left-hand side lies Lacock Abbey. In ¼ mile, beyond a raised causeway and the river Avon, cross a stone slab stile on the left to enter an open field. Head directly across this first open field to a telegraph pole in the opposite hedgerow, following the direction indicated by the marker post

37

Medieval Lacock

alongside the stile. At the far side of this field, cross a stile and bear left along the edge of the next field to a stile just 40 yards away. Head directly across a third field, following the telegraph wires, to a stile on the far side.

2. Cross this stile, and drop down to the banks of the Avon. Follow the riverbank upstream across two fields, before crossing a stile alongside an attractive stone bridge in the hamlet of Reybridge. To the right is another raised causeway, which keeps the pavement high and dry when the river is in flood.

3. Turn left and cross the river, before turning left at a junction in front of an attractive thatched cottage. In just a few yards, where the road bears right, keep directly ahead along a tarmac path that runs between a pair of stone cottages. Shortly, this path passes a kissing gate to enter an open field. Follow what is still a tarmac path across the middle of the field, with the Avon below on the left set against a backdrop of Naish Hill and Bowden Hill.

At the far side of the field, pass through another kissing gate and turn left to follow a back lane down into Lacock. The path crosses

Bide Brook on an attractive footbridge – the lane passing through a ford on the left – before reaching St Cyriac's church in Lacock.

4. Turn right by the church, and walk the length of Church Street to its junction with West Street, admiring along the way a number of attractive brick and thatch houses. Turn left along West Street, passing the George Inn, before turning left into the High Street. Continue along the High Street, its width reflecting its former use for markets and fairs, until you reach the Red Lion on the right-hand side.

To return to your car, continue along the Devizes road out of Lacock. Immediately past the entrance to Lacock Abbey, follow a gravel path on the right that runs parallel to the road. This path soon passes through a small copse before emerging at the entrance to the car park in Hither Way.

PLACES OF INTEREST NEARBY
The Fox Talbot Museum, housed in a 16th-century barn by the gates to *Lacock Abbey,* is dedicated to the founding father of photography (telephone 01249 730459). The abbey itself preserves a few monastic fragments amid the 18th-century Gothic (telephone 01249 730227).

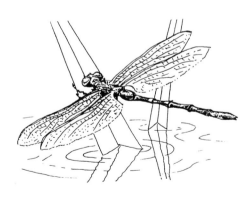

THE SOMERSET FROME AT RODE

There can be few families in the Bath and Bristol area who have not enjoyed a visit to the Tropical Bird Gardens at Rode. Just below this major attraction, the Frome Valley provides a delightful setting for this walk through a quiet corner of Somerset to the neighbouring village of Tellisford.

Tellisford Bridge

The river Frome flows from the Somerset town of the same name to join the Bristol Avon at Freshford. In years gone by, the West of England woollen trade made full use of the river's water power with a number of mills being located along its course. At both Rode and Tellisford, old mill buildings in various states of repair lie alongside the river. The mill at Tellisford, for example, dates from 1574 and was worked by a Trowbridge clothing family.

Heading out of Rode initially involves following the river bank itself. Popular with local anglers, trout are often to be seen in the

Frome's clear waters. Alongside the weir in Tellisford lies a wartime pill box. Imaginations can run riot at the thought of the invading German army paddling its way down the river towards Bath and Bristol! Just down the river from this military antiquity lies Tellisford Bridge, a delightful footbridge that will prove irresistible for lovers of a game of Pooh Sticks.

The return to Rode follows the hillsides to the west of the Frome. The views across the valley towards the fringes of Salisbury Plain are particularly memorable, although the eye will inevitably be drawn to the church on the skyline on the fringes of Rode. Dating from 1824, Christ Church is a cacophony of pinnacles that was described by Pevsner as 'amazing'.

Back in Rode, another former mill building has been converted into a fine restaurant and bar. The Mill Inn dates back to the 11th century, and is mentioned in the Domesday Book. Originally a cloth mill, which at one time produced uniforms for the Napoleonic War, trade declined during the Industrial Revolution as textile production shifted to the coalfields of northern England. The 19th century saw a change of use to a corn mill, with flour being produced for local residents. The 20th century saw the mill drift into a period of a gentle decay, before the site was purchased in 1991 for conversion to an attractive restaurant and bar.

The food at the Mill includes a good range of baguettes, light bites and bigger bites. There are such tempting baguette options as prawn, bacon, tuna or cheese, whilst the light bites include avocado and bacon salad served with potato wedges, king prawns in filo pastry with salad garnish and garlic dip and smoked chicken and bacon salad with potato wedges. Perhaps the best place to enjoy your food and drink is in the garden area overlooking the river Frome. Excellent food, a good West Country beer such as Wadworth 6X and a riverside setting make the perfect combination.

Telephone: 01373 831096.

- **HOW TO GET THERE:** Follow the A36 south from Bath for 10 miles to the village of Woolverton, before turning left along the unclassified road signposted to Rode. Cross Rode Bridge – alongside which is located the Mill Inn – and climb Rode Hill before turning right into Rode's High Street, the turning just before Christ Church.

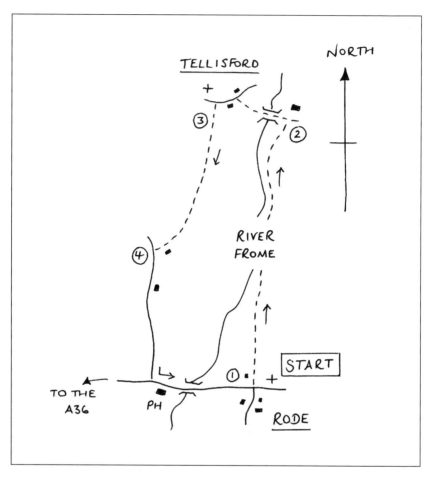

- **PARKING:** Park carefully in the High Street, as near to the junction with the Woolverton road as possible.
- **LENGTH OF THE WALK:** 2¹/₂ miles. Maps: OS Landranger 173 Swindon and Devizes and 183 Yeovil and Frome or OS Explorer 143 Warminster and Trowbridge (GR 805542).

THE WALK

1. At the northern end of the High Street in Rode, by the village hall, the High Street joins the road leading from Rode to Woolverton. Cross over this road, and follow the lane opposite – signposted 'Langham Place numbers 1–3' – that runs to the right of Langham House. In 100 yards, cross a cattle grid and follow the tarmac drive ahead across the field towards Langham Farm. In 1/4 mile, beyond the parking area for the local angling club, the drive becomes an unmetalled track. Continue along this track to Langham Farm, keeping left at a prominent fork just above the river Frome.

Pass to the right of the farmhouse, following the track which ends at a gateway and an open field. Cross the first field, following the river Frome on the left downstream, to a stile at the far side of the field. Continue following the Frome downstream in the next field, passing a magnificent weir on the left. At the far side of this second field, cross a metal stile just to the right of the river, to join the path coming down Vagg's Hill to the hamlet of Tellisford.

2. Turn left and cross the picturesque footbridge across the Frome. Continue following the path as it climbs the hillside past the attractive cottages and houses of Tellisford. Beyond Crabb Cottage, continue along the lane out of Tellisford. Just past the last cottage on the left in Tellisford – Lilac Cottage – cross a stile on the left.

3. Over the stile, follow the signposted footpath into an open field. Cross to the far left-hand corner of this field, dropping down the hillside along the way, to a stile. Along the way, fine views open up on the left across the Frome Valley.

In the next field, bear right to climb the slope and follow the field boundary at the top of the hill behind a small copse to a stile in the far corner of the field. Follow the right edge of the next field to a gap in the hedge in the far right corner. Head directly across the next field to a stile, 40 yards opposite, before continuing across the right edge of the next two fields high above the river Frome.

In the corner of the last field, turn right through a gateway to follow an enclosed farm track. In about 100 yards, bear left off this track to a stile. Beyond the stile, head directly across an open field, passing a bungalow on the left, to a stile in the far right-hand corner of the field.

4. Join the Tellisford to Rode lane, and turn left. In 200 yards, you reach a junction, with the Mill Inn opposite. Turn left, cross Rode Bridge and follow Rode Hill for 200 yards to return to Rode High Street, which lies on the right just before Rode church.

THE RIVER AVON AND THE KENNET & AVON CANAL AT BRADFORD-ON-AVON

Enjoy a leisurely stroll in a secluded corner of the Avon Valley where the river runs cheek by jowl with the K & A Canal. Along the way, discover colourful narrow-boats, a rich array of wildfowl, a magnificent aqueduct and one of England's finest small towns.

Bradford Wharf

The isolated hamlet of Avoncliff, 6 miles south-east of Bath, lies in one of the most out-of-the-way parts of the Avon Valley. With narrow cul-de-sac lanes from Westwood and Bradford providing the only road access, weekend visitors are a thorn in the flesh of local residents. Avoncliff Aqueduct, the K & A Canal, the Cross Guns Inn and the river Avon act as a magnet, attracting large numbers of vehicles seeking out the score or so parking places.

A more pleasant way of visiting this beauty spot is to enjoy a walk through the Barton Farm Country Park from nearby Bradford-on-Avon. A $1\frac{1}{2}$ mile stroll along the banks of the Avon makes that pint at the Cross Guns particularly welcome, with the return along the K & A towpath providing a glimpse into the life of this recently restored waterway.

Avoncliff is of particular interest to the industrial archaeologist, being a settlement founded on the local stone and woollen industries. The quarry tramline down to the canal from Westwood has long disappeared, although a ruinous flock mill still stands alongside the weir on the Avon.

The Saxon town of Bradford-on-Avon has been responsible for the launch of any number of postcards, television programmes, books and magazine features. It is easy to see why the town has been described as 'a clone of Bath'. The Saxon church, the lock-up on the town bridge, the vast tithe barn and the many fine buildings fashioned from the local stone make Bradford an architect's delight, the jewel in the crown of this delightful walk through the Avon Valley.

The Cross Guns Inn at Avoncliff sits conveniently at the halfway point on this walk. Dating from the 17th century, this was the watering hole of local weavers long before the K & A Canal turned the inn into a bargees' pub in the late 18th century. The location of the Cross Guns, sandwiched quite literally between the K & A and the river Avon, makes it an ever popular hostelry, with today's customers being a mix of walkers, cyclists, locals enjoying a pleasant few hours in the countryside, as well as the passing boat trade.

This is a marvellously old-fashioned pub, with a vast stone fireplace, stone walls, low beams and solid oak tables. The bar area can become very crowded, but this is not a problem – on the terraces and lawn in front of the inn are any number of picnic tables overlooking the river Avon and the local aqueduct that carries the K & A across the river. A quite delightful spot in which to enjoy some fine home cooking. The food on offer ranges from sandwiches and ploughman's through to substantial offerings such as steak and kidney pie, lemon sole, duck in orange sauce and a good range of steaks. With fine local beers, such as Mole's, Smiles and Ushers, usually available, this excellent hostelry complements perfectly what is an exceptional walk in the Avon Valley.

Telephone: 01225 862335.

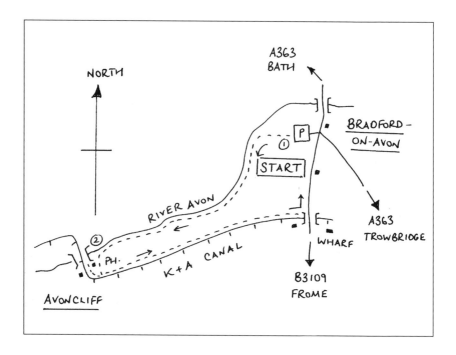

- **HOW TO GET THERE:** Follow the A4 eastwards from Bath to Bathford before turning onto the A363 road signposted to Bradford-on-Avon. It is a 6 mile drive from Bathford into Bradford.
- **PARKING:** In the centre of Bradford-on-Avon, park in the signposted station car park (fee payable).
- **LENGTH OF THE WALK:** 3 miles. Maps: OS Landranger 173 Swindon and Devizes or OS Explorer 156 Chippenham (GR 824607).

THE WALK

1. Walk to the far end of the station car park before following the path that drops downhill, bearing left under the railway bridge beside the river Avon. Continue along this gravelled path as it crosses a grassed recreation area by the river, before joining a tarmac path just by the complex of old buildings that make up Barton Farm. Continue along this tarmac path, with the river on the right-hand side.

In just under ½ mile, where the tarmac path bears left to climb uphill to the K & A Canal, continue following the grassy riverside path that borders the river Avon. Continue along this path as it

The old mill, Bradford

passes through a gateway to enter an open field. Follow the fieldpath ahead across four fields, all the while bordering the river Avon.

2. At the far side of the fourth field, the path reaches Avoncliff Weir. Turn left at this point, and climb the steps up to the towpath alongside the K & A Canal. A short detour to the right will enable you to explore Avoncliff, with its aqueduct, cottages, tea-rooms and pub.

Turn left along the towpath to continue the main walk. Follow the towpath for 1¹/₄ miles back to the B3109 Frome Road in Bradford by the Canal Tavern. A short detour to the right will soon bring you to Bradford Lock and Wharf. To continue the main walk, turn left along the main road for ¹/₄ mile, where a left turn at the mini-roundabout by Stones Garage will bring you back to the station car park.

THE AVON VALLEY
SOUTH OF BATH

Between Bath and Bradford-on-Avon lies the most spectacular section of the Avon Valley. Steep, wooded hillsides come tumbling down to the river bank, which runs cheek by jowl with the Kennet & Avon Canal. It is not difficult to see why this is one of the most popular walking destinations in the area.

The Kennet & Avon Canal at Dundas

South of Bath, the river Avon flows through what is arguably the finest natural landscape in the Bath and Bristol area. Steep, wooded hillsides rise for over 400 feet above the valley bottom, hills formed of golden limestone. The various means of communication that cling together along the valley floor tell the complete human history of transport from footpaths and rivers, through the canal and railway eras to the modern motor age.

This walk begins at Dundas Wharf, the junction of the K & A Canal with the Somerset Coal Canal. The canal ran from the mines around Paulton and Radstock to Dundas, and in its heyday carried upwards of 150,000 tons of coal each year. Alongside Dundas Wharf stands Dundas Aqueduct, regarded as the finest in Southern England. Its central semi-circular arch carries the K & A across the river Avon, whilst the smaller outside arches carry the waterway across a footpath and the Bristol to Southampton railway respectively.

From this exceptional canalside scene, the walk climbs the steep hillside to the east of the canal to reach the remote hilltop hamlet of Conkwell, a former quarry settlement that is now a rural idyll for harassed city commuters. From Conkwell, quiet lanes are followed through Warleigh Woods down to Sheephouse Farm, deep in the heart of the Avon Valley. Below Sheephouse Farm lies the river itself, and the waterside meadows that are followed back to Dundas. Along the way, keep your eyes scanned for the wildfowl that make their home in this corner of the valley. As well as the ubiquitous mallard and moorhen, solitary herons are residents of the valley.

On the main A36 just above Dundas Wharf stands the Viaduct Inn, named after the handsome stone viaduct that carries the main road southwards towards Warminster and Frome. The inn sign depicts a horse and carriage from a bygone era crossing this most impressive of constructions. The Viaduct Inn boasts a whole range of attractions for customers, including all day opening, good food, a skittle alley, function room, beer garden with great views and B & B. The bottom line, however, is that the Viaduct Inn is a good old-fashioned pub that provides an extensive range of straightforward food, as well as fine Ushers beers, brewed just down the road in Trowbridge.

All of the usual pub staples are available at the Viaduct Inn, including sandwiches, ploughman's, baguettes and soup, as well as fish dishes, chicken, steaks, grills and salads. Meals can be enjoyed in the eating-only section of the main bar, which lies on the left-hand side as you enter the inn. To accompany your meal, Ushers Best Bitter or Founders Ale come highly recommended. Ushers also brew their Four Seasons Ales, a range of short-term cask beers which aim to reflect the season and the cereals harvested at that time. If the sun is shining, refreshment can be enjoyed in the beer garden at the back of the Viaduct Inn, with its fine views across the Avon Valley.

Telephone: 01225 723187.

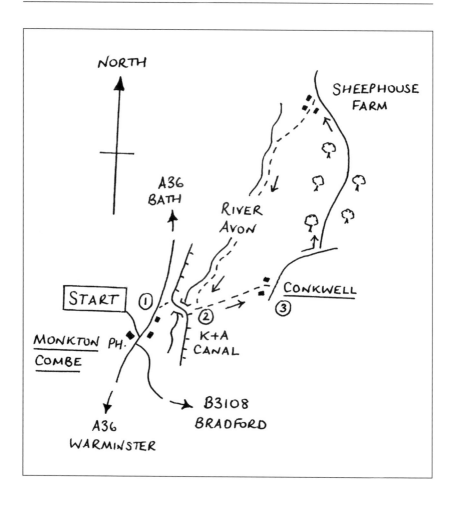

- **HOW TO GET THERE:** Follow the A36 Warminster road south from Bath for 5 miles. Just before the Monkton Combe Garage and the B3108 left turn to Bradford-on-Avon, there is a layby on the left-hand side of the A36. The Viaduct Inn lies at the junction of the A36 with the B3108, and is just a short drive or walk from the layby at the end of the walk.
- **PARKING:** For the walk, park in the layby described above. There is a car park alongside the Viaduct Inn for patrons of the pub.
- **LENGTH OF THE WALK:** 3 miles. Maps: OS Landranger 172 Bristol and Bath or OS Explorer 155 Bristol and Bath (GR 784625).

Avoncliff Aqueduct

THE WALK

1. Follow the stepped footpath at the Bath end of the layby down to Dundas Wharf. Turn left on reaching the canal, walking past a restored crane and warehouse to a white footbridge – number 177 – and across the K & A. Turn right, and follow the towpath across Dundas Aqueduct. At the far side of this magnificent construction, continue ahead behind a large wooden shed to reach a stile and a track that climbs into Conkwell Wood. The track marks the course of an old mineral tramline that brought limestone from the hilltop quarries down to the wharf.

2. Follow the track for just a few yards, before turning left into an open hillside field. There is a faint yellow arrow on a marker stone, but this is easily missed. Cross this hillside field diagonally, climbing to a stile in the top right-hand corner, all the while enjoying magnificent views northwards along the Avon Valley. Cross this stile, and bear right to reach the top corner of the next field. At the top of this field, continue along a boulder-strewn track uphill, past another stile, into Conkwell. Follow the tarmac path up through this diminutive hamlet to a lane at the top of the hill.

3. Turn left and follow the lane away from Conkwell for 300 yards to a road junction. Turn left, and follow the lane signposted to Warleigh and Bathford. Follow this lane through Warleigh Wood. Very little traffic passes this way, making this section of the walk a very pleasant woodland stroll. In $3/4$ mile, the lane begins to descend the hillside steeply, before reaching two consecutive driveways on the left-hand side. Ignore the first driveway leading to Tanglewood, taking instead the second left turn leading into Sheephouse Farm.

4. Pass through the farm buildings to a gateway at the far end of the farmyard. Just before this gate, bear right and follow an enclosed footpath downhill for 30 yards to a stile above the Avon Valley. Cross this stile, and follow the fence beyond downhill for 15 yards to another stile on the left. Beyond this stile, follow a sloping hillside path downhill towards the river Avon.

5. In the far right-hand corner of this hillside field, by the river, cross a footbridge and a stile to reach the waterside meadows. Follow the river upstream across four fields until you arrive back at Dundas Aqueduct. Pass to the left of the Monkton Combe School Rowing Club, which lies below the aqueduct, and follow a stepped path back up to the canal. Turn right, cross the aqueduct, and retrace your steps back around Dundas Wharf and up that stepped path to the layby. It is now just a short walk or car ride down the A36 to the Viaduct Inn.

PLACES OF INTEREST NEARBY
At nearby Claverton is the *American Museum and Gardens*. Housed in a former manor house, visitors can experience the way in which Americans lived between the 17th and 19th centuries. Telephone the American Museum on 01225 460503 for details. Alongside Dundas Wharf is the *Bath & Dundas Canal Company* where, in addition to boat hire on the K&A Canal, there is a visitors display which relates to the Somerset Coal Canal. Telephone 01225 722292 for details.

THE WELLOW BROOK

Explore a delightful slice of North Somerset countryside, where a picture postcard village nestles on a hillside above a sparkling brook.

The ford at Wellow

The hills to the south of Bath separate a series of delightful valleys, each of which carries its own tributary stream down to the river Avon. The village of Wellow sits proudly above Wellow Brook, crossed at the foot of Mill Hill by a ford and a medieval packhorse bridge. It is a spot where many a passing walker leans on the old bridge to watch the occasional passing car ploughing slowly through the water below.

Wellow Brook has its source in the Eastern Mendips, originating in the springs that lie dotted around Ston Easton Park. It flows eastwards through the former mining town of Radstock and on to Wellow, before joining up with Midford Brook in Midford itself. Its clear waters should make it possible to spot the trout that are

53

synonymous with the Avon's tributaries south of Bath.

The village of Wellow is a pleasant blend of stone cottages and houses centred on the village square and the Fox and Badger Inn. Along the main street from the hostelry stands the pride of the village, St Julian's church, a sturdy Perpendicular building with a fine west tower.

Railway enthusiasts may be familiar with the name Wellow, a stop on the former Somerset and Dorset Railway that ran the 71 miles from Bath to Bournemouth. The old S & D – 'serene and delightful' to its many friends, but 'slow and dirty' to its critics – survived for over a century until it fell victim to the Beeching cuts in 1966. The railway may be long gone, but a rather impressive viaduct greets visitors approaching Wellow from Hinton Charterhouse, whilst a restored signal box lies down the lane alongside the village pub.

Lovely though these collections of stone and mortar are, it is the natural beauty of the landscape that will remain with the visitor. The deep valley, the quiet riverside paths and the far-ranging views combine to produce a panorama that has been described as 'almost too English to be true'.

English through and through is the local hostelry, the Fox and Badger. Fashioned from local stone, the inn sign depicting a fox and a badger dressed Regency style will soon catch the eye of visitors passing through the village square. With its hanging baskets and exterior bench seats, the Fox and Badger is certainly a prominent village landmark.

Internally, this traditional hostelry contains a public bar and a lounge, the bar offering a good selection of old pub games including table skittles and dominoes. Flagstone flooring, open fireplaces and wooden beams lend a rustic feel to the inn, providing a decor that is complemented by cushioned settles and displays of china, copper and brass.

After a waterside walk beside the Wellow Brook, appetites can be satisfied at the Fox and Badger from a good selection of dishes displayed on boards in the bar. These might include trout, steak pie, Cumberland sausages or pork kebabs, as well as lighter snacks and meals such as smoked mackerel, Cheddar ploughman's or beef sandwiches. A good selection of drinks is also available at the inn, including Butcombe, Wadworth 6X and Thatcher's farm cider, as well as a regular guest ale.

Telephone: 01225 832293.

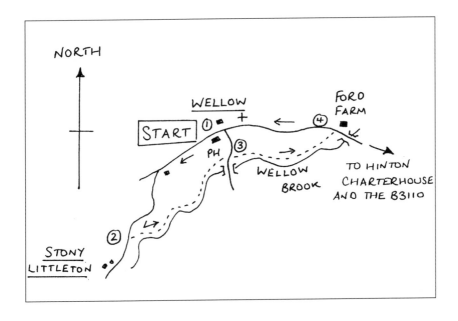

- **HOW TO GET THERE:** The B3110 running south from Bath to Norton St Philip passes through Hinton Charterhouse. Leave the B3110 at this point to follow the unclassified road signposted to Wellow. In just over 2 miles, this road passes beneath the arches of the old Somerset and Dorset Railway viaduct before climbing into Wellow.
- **PARKING:** There is room for roadside parking in the centre of Wellow, in the vicinity of the Fox and Badger Inn.
- **LENGTH OF THE WALK:** 3 miles. Maps: OS Landranger 172 Bristol and Bath and OS Explorer 5 Mendip Hills East (GR 739583).

THE WALK

1. Follow the main street in Wellow westwards, away from the Fox and Badger and the village square in the direction of Peasedown. In a little over ¼ mile, on the edge of the village, turn left along the lane signposted to Stony Littleton Long Barrow. Follow this quiet byway for almost ½ mile, all the while enjoying views across the local countryside, until you reach a stile on the left-hand side and a signposted public footpath.

The village pub

2. Cross the stile, and you will straightaway hear and see Wellow Brook down on the right. Follow Wellow Brook downstream across three fields, keeping to the river bank. Stiles in the field boundaries at the end of each field mark the course of the right-of-way. At the far side of the third field, follow the path as it rises to a stile. Cross this stile, and you will join a gravelled path. Turn right, and follow this path downhill to the packhorse bridge on the edge of Wellow.

3. Immediately before the bridge, turn left in front of a cottage, and cross the lane and the stile opposite into a meadow by Wellow Brook. Follow the brook downstream across a further four fields, the fields to your left housing many of the horses used at the nearby Wellow Trekking Centre.

4. At the far side of the fourth field, bear left away from Wellow Brook to a stile by Ford Farm which brings you onto Ford Road. Turn left, and follow this lane for ½ mile back into Wellow, passing along the way the local trekking centre, the Somerset and Dorset Railway viaduct and St Julian's church. Just past the church, the lane emerges into the village square by the Fox and Badger Inn.

THE WATERWAYS OF BATH

The Roman Baths, magnificent Georgian architecture and a splendid abbey make Bath one of Europe's finest small cities. Combine a visit to the city with this idyllic stroll along the river Avon and the Kennet & Avon Canal, and you have the makings of a perfect day out.

Bath Abbey from across the Avon

The City of Bath, famous for its Roman Baths and elegant Georgian architecture, marks the point at which the Kennet & Avon Canal officially leaves the river Avon. A flight of six locks carries the K & A up and out of the city, through the secluded and shady Sydney Gardens. In order to blend in with these delightful surroundings, the canal company had to construct a pair of intricate iron footbridges across the canal, as well as ensuring that the entrances to the Sydney Gardens Tunnel were formed of ornately carved and decorated Bath stone.

57

This short walk also includes a stroll along Great Pulteney Street, one of the most magnificent Georgian streets to be found in Britain, together with a riverside walk along the banks of the Avon downstream of Pulteney Bridge and the famous Horseshoe Falls. This is altogether a quite superb town-trail that will leave you in no doubt as to why visitors have been flocking to this most beautiful of cities for close on 2,000 years.

One of Bath's lesser known attractions lies almost at journey's end – the Old Green Tree pub in Green Street. An interesting story lies behind the name of this most traditional of pubs. At one time, it was claimed that Bathonians could see the trees on the hills surrounding their city from every pub in the town with the exception of this small hostelry in one of the city centre's narrow side streets. The landlord, not wishing to be left out on a limb, planted a tree in the backyard so that his customers would not be denied the sight of a tree whilst enjoying their pint of ale. Hence the name – the Old Green Tree. Today's hostelry consists of three oak-panelled small rooms, including a pleasant lounge decorated with wartime aircraft pictures.

A good range of regular bar food is offered here, as well as an ever changing number of daily specials. The regular choices include soup, filled baps, ploughman's, salads, bangers and mash and curries, whilst the specials have included faggots with onion gravy and mash, pesto pasta and beef rogan josh. The Old Green Tree is perhaps better known, however, for being a fine real ale pub. Local beers regularly feature at the bar, and these have included Oakhill Black Magic, Uley Hogshead and Wickwar Brand Oak Bitter. Altogether a most traditional, unspoilt pub, that will provide a friendly welcome at the end of this fine waterside walk in Bath. Telephone: 01225 448259.

- **HOW TO GET THERE:** Turn off the A4 onto the A3039 Walcot Street, 1/4 mile west of the junction of the A4 with the A36 in the centre of Bath. Towards the bottom of Walcot Street, park in the signposted Walcot Street car park (fee payable).
- **PARKING:** See above. As an alternative, two-hour parking is allowed on Walcot Street itself between 9 am and 6 pm, Mondays to Saturdays. Parking vouchers can be purchased from local retail outlets. Better still, do the walk on a Sunday when Bath is much quieter and parking is free.

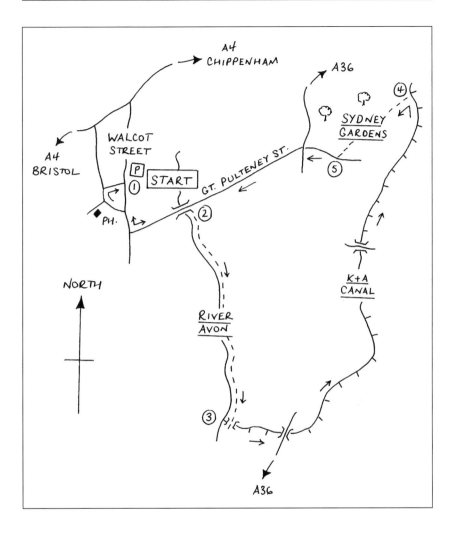

- **LENGTH OF THE WALK:** 2¹/₂ miles. Maps: OS Landranger 172 Bristol and Bath or OS Explorer 155 Bristol and Bath (GR 751653).

THE WALK

1. Leave the car park and turn left along Walcot Street. When you reach the junction of Walcot Street and Broad Street, St Michael with St Paul church on your right, continue ahead along the High Street walking in the direction of Bath Abbey. In 75 yards, turn left into Bridge Street and continue directly ahead across Pulteney Bridge.

59

2. At the far side of Pulteney Bridge, turn immediately right to descend a flight of steps to reach the signposted Riverside Walk. At the foot of these steps, follow the Avon downstream for 1/2 mile, passing beneath North Parade Bridge and a railway bridge along the way. The Riverside Walk follows a tarmac path for most of the way, although there is a short section of road walking by the river between North Parade Bridge and the railway.

3. Just before reaching the main A36, the path crosses the Kennet & Avon Canal at Widcombe Bridge, alongside the junction of the K&A with the Avon. Go over the canal and turn left to follow the K&A away from the river. Follow the towpath past the Bath Stakis Hotel, pass under a pair of road bridges and climb a flight of steps to reach Bath Bottom Lock. The towpath now switches to the other bank of the canal, and is reached by crossing a plank walkway on the bottom set of lock gates.

Follow the towpath up through Widcombe Locks for 1/2 mile, crossing one road along the way, until you reach Bathwick Hill. At Bathwick Hill, climb a flight of steps on the left, cross the road, and follow the path opposite back down to the canal, with the towpath having changed banks once again. Continue along the towpath for 1/4 mile until you reach Cleveland House. Cross the canal in front of Cleveland House, and pass through Cleveland Tunnel.

4. At the far end of the tunnel, pass beneath an ornate footbridge before turning left through a gateway into Sydney Gardens. Follow the tarmac path ahead over the railway and in front of a stone temple-like park shelter, before bearing left to follow the path on through the park and out into Sydney Place.

5. Turn right, walk down Sydney Place to the A36 and cross over into Great Pulteney Street. Walk the length of this magnificent Georgian street to Laura Place, and continue ahead to cross Pulteney Bridge. Keep on along Bridge Street to the High Street, and turn right to reach St Michael with St Paul church. Keep left at the church, walking up Broad Street. Almost immediately, Green Street with the Green Tree pub is on the left. To return to Walcot Street, continue along Broad Street for a short distance before turning right along Saracen Street. This brings you back to Walcot Street, where a left turn will soon return you to the car park.

THE RIVER AVON AT SWINEFORD

At their southernmost point, the Cotswold Hills come tumbling down towards the banks of the Avon. It was in this picturesque location that a herd of pigs once experienced a miraculous cure!

Sailing on the Avon

The legendary Prince Bladud was at one time banished to Keynsham, midway between Bath and Bristol, on account of his leprosy. Working as a swineherd, he passed on his disease to an unfortunate herd of pigs. While he was driving the herd across the Avon at a local ford one day, the pigs panicked. They swam upstream to Bath and were cured of their leprosy as they struggled through a morass of mud. Bladud tried the remedy with similar success, and built baths over the curative springs for which Bath subsequently became famous.

Swineford, a few miles west of Bath, marks the spot where Bladud attempted to drive his pigs across the river. The village is the start of this walk, which explores an area where the Cotswold Hills come down towards the Avon. From the village picnic area, a quiet footpath climbs the hillside to North Stoke. This isolated village is full of beautiful old buildings, including St Martin's church and the double-gabled Manor House Farm.

Below the village lies the hamlet of Kelston Mills. Brass-making gave birth to this settlement back in the 1760s, although the outer walls of two furnace chimneys and a row of workers' cottages are the only relics of this industry. The walk back to Swineford then follows riverside footpaths and a section of the Railway Path, a recreational right-of-way that follows the course of the former Midland Railway between Bath and Bristol. The Avon hereabouts is navigable, and 'messing about on the river', as well as angling, are popular weekend pastimes.

Alongside the Railway Path lies the Bird-in-Hand pub. This hostelry was originally set up in the 19th century to serve the navvies working on the railway. Constructed of the local stone, much of which has now disappeared beneath a coat of whitewash, the Bird-in-Hand has been extensively modernised in recent years.

A substantial menu is available at the Bird-in-Hand, which ranges from filled rolls, jacket potatoes and platters, through to more extensive offerings such as beef and ale pie, mushroom stroganoff and ham, egg and chips. In addition, a number of special dishes are prepared each day. These might include Somerset pork in cider, traditional roast beef and cauliflower cheese. The desserts are difficult to resist, and include apple pie, spotted dick and death by chocolate.

Well-known beers such as Courage Best and Bass are served here, as well as ales from local breweries such as Abbey Ale from Bath, Mole's from Melksham and Smiles from Bristol. Halfway around this stroll through the Avon Valley, the best place to enjoy a pint is either on the inn's patio, or in the rear garden with its fishpond. Telephone: 01125 873335.

- **HOW TO GET THERE:** Swineford lies on the A431 between Bath and Bristol.
- **PARKING:** Park in the signposted picnic area, just west of the Swan public house.
- **LENGTH OF THE WALK:** 4 miles. Maps: OS Landranger 172 Bristol and Bath or OS Explorer 155 Bristol and Bath (GR 691692).

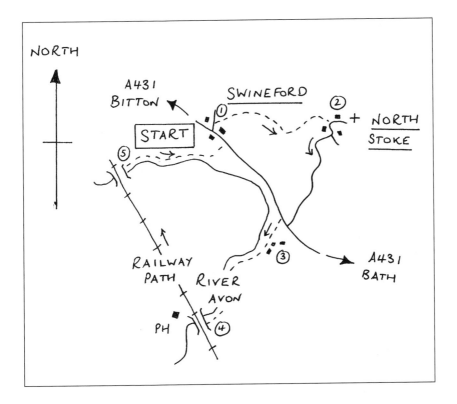

THE WALK

1. As you enter the picnic area, look out for a footpath signposted on the right-hand side. Follow this path, crossing a stile to enter an open field. Continue along a well-worn fieldpath uphill across two fields to reach a stile at the top of the second field. Beyond this stile, follow an enclosed path on into the hilltop village of North Stoke.

2. On reaching the road in North Stoke, just past a collection of farm buildings, turn right and follow the road through the village. On the edge of the village, at a road junction, keep right and follow a lane downhill to the A431. On reaching the main road, turn right and, in just 40 yards, follow a signposted footpath on the left across a stile into an open field. Cross the left edge of the field, the Avon to the right, to a stile in the far left corner. In the next field, follow the right edge towards the hamlet of Kelston Mills.

The Bird in Hand pub alongside the Railway Path

3. Cross a stile just before these cottages, continue down to a lane and bear right to a rank of former workers' cottages. Pass in front of these cottages to a stile, before bearing right down to the river Avon. On reaching the river, turn left and follow the Avon upstream across three fields. Halfway across the third field, cross a stile on the right before following a stepped path on the left up to the Railway Path.

4. Turn right and follow the Railway Path westwards across the Avon. Having crossed the river, you will see the Bird-in-Hand pub down the steps on the left-hand side. For the walk itself, continue following the Railway Path westwards for 1 mile to the next bridge across the Avon. Just beyond this bridge, follow a rough stepped path on the left down to the riverbank. Turn left on reaching the river, and follow a path under the bridge beneath the Railway Path.

5. Continue following the river upstream across three fields. In the third field, the path bears left away from the Avon to follow a millstream up towards the main A431 and the clearly visible Swan Inn at Swineford. Cross a stile in front of the pub, turn left along the A431 before turning right to follow the lane back to the picnic area.

THE RIVER AVON NEAR KEYNSHAM

A vivid imagination will conjure up images of an industrial past on this leisurely ramble through the Avon Valley. The sound of riotous miners has long since passed, with the river now echoing to little more than the sound of the occasional passing pleasure craft.

Keynsham marina

Despite the proximity of both Bath and Bristol, the Avon Valley between Keynsham and Swineford still manages to exude a certain rural charm. Holm Mead, the pasture to the north of the river, is set against a fine backdrop of hills that mark the southern end of the Cotswolds. Kelston Round Hill is a notable landmark, as is the diminutive hamlet of North Stoke, nestling below Lansdown Hill.

The Avon between Bath and Bristol was not always a navigable waterway. It was only in 1727 that the Avon Navigation was officially opened, enabling the first cargo of deal boards, pig lead and metal to reach Bath. Subsequent cargoes of Shropshire coal were less welcome, with local miners destroying Saltford Lock in response to what was seen as a threat to their livelihoods.

Ironically, the Avon Navigation enabled locally produced coal to reach a wider market. The Avon & Gloucestershire Railway, a horse-drawn tramway, ran from collieries near Mangotsfield to the river at Keynsham. Traces of the tramway embankment and the site of Avon Wharf can be found just east of Avondale House on this walk, together with a former stable and weighbridge.

A more recent rail link also forms part of this walk. The Midland Railway running from Mangotsfield to Bath Green Park is followed for $3/4$ mile. A victim of the Beeching cuts in the 1960s, the track has now become the Bristol and Bath Railway Path. The line, which once echoed to the sound of the Pines Express en route from Manchester to Bournemouth, was the first major cyclepath project in Britain when construction commenced in 1969.

At journey's end, alongside the Avon Navigation, lies the Lock Keeper Inn. Standing above County Lock, this waterside hostelry is proving increasingly popular with both local residents and passing boat-owners. The Lock Keeper has a very traditional feel, with its exposed boards, cushioned settles, wooden tables and beamed ceilings. Around the walls are displayed a number of old black-and-white photographs that feature riverside scenes as well as the inn itself. Lending an element of interest to the bar area are the various objects hanging from the ceiling. These include a pram, an old umbrella, clogs, keep nets, paddles and a branch laden with hops.

Blackboards in the bar are used to display the day's menu. In addition to the standard fare of baguettes, jacket potatoes, ploughman's and French sticks, various specials are available each day. These range from home-made soup through to more substantial offerings such as pan-fried salmon with a dill sauce. Desserts, such as apple pie and chocolate fudge cake, will probably prove irresistible, as will a pint of locally brewed Smiles beer. This Bristol-based brewery owns the Lock Keeper, and brews such as Smiles Golden and Heritage are highly recommended.

Telephone: 0117 986 2383.

● **HOW TO GET THERE:** Just $1/2$ mile north of Keynsham on the A4175 Bitton road, turn right onto the side road leading to the Lock Keeper Inn. The inn lies at the end of what is a short cul-de-sac lane.

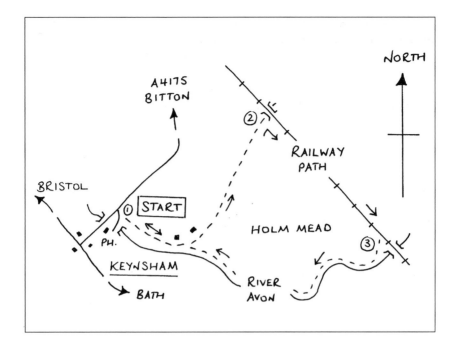

- **PARKING:** There is a public car park on the right just before the Lock Keeper. The inn itself also has an extensive parking area alongside the river Avon.
- **LENGTH OF THE WALK:** 3$^1/_2$ miles. Maps: OS Landranger 172 Bristol and Bath or OS Explorer 155 Bristol and Bath (GR 660690).

THE WALK

1. Follow the signposted footpath opposite the Lock Keeper Inn. This initially passes the local marina before following the banks of the Avon for $^1/_4$ mile to reach a cattle grid alongside a bungalow. Continue ahead along the gravel track, away from the river, towards Avondale House. Where the drive bears left to the house itself, continue ahead across the field to a stile alongside a gate. Follow the left-hand field boundary across the next two fields.

At the end of the second field, cross a stile on the left and continue along the opposite side of the hedgerow to another stile. In the next field, aim for a stile in the opposite hedgerow 30 yards to the left of an old stone building. Cross this stile, turn left and follow the field boundary for 200 yards around to the Railway Path.

67

Waiting to start the walk!

2. Climb the steps up the embankment to the former trackbed, which is followed to the right for $3/4$ mile. The raised elevation enjoyed by the Railway Path brings extensive views across the Avon Valley. Just before an old railway bridge across the Avon, descend some steps on the right to reach the river bank.

3. Follow the river to the right back towards Keynsham. Just beyond the cattle grid passed at the outset, bear left and leave the gravel track to follow the riverside path back to the Lock Keeper.

PLACES OF INTEREST NEARBY

On the fringes of Keynsham lies the *Avon Valley Country Park*, a river-based park that includes a range of attractions including exotic – but friendly – animals, a children's assault course, boating, mini-golf, pets corner and fishing. For further details, telephone 0117 986 4929.

WALK 15

BRISTOL'S HISTORIC DOCKS

Bristol's Floating Harbour is a unique blend of history, nostalgia and charm. Motor yachts, river cruisers and barges sit cheek by jowl where once ocean-going steamships and cargo vessels plied their trade.

The river Avon at Bristol

Bristol's wealth and prosperity can be traced historically to the city's great seafaring tradition. The slave trade, a shameful chapter in Bristol's history, forged links with the West Indies and the Americas. Out of these links grew many of the city's historic industries – tobacco, sugar, chocolate and sherry being some examples.

This seafaring tradition was brought right to the heart of the city by way of the navigable river Avon. Although the old City Docks can no longer accommodate today's vast sea-going vessels, the old quays and wharves in the city centre still convey the atmosphere of a historic seaport.

In the 19th century, Bristol's fortunes as a port declined due to the tides that handicapped navigation on the Avon. In an attempt to revive the port's fortunes, lock gates were installed at either end of what became known as the 'Floating Harbour', and a 'New Cut' was dug to carry the tidal waters of the Avon to the south of the port.

This walk explores the city's Floating Harbour, now a vast leisure amenity, as well as following a stretch of the New Cut. Away from the water's edge, our steps follow the cobbles of King Street. It takes very little imagination to step back in time and imagine King Street as the setting for the start of Robert Louis Stevenson's *Treasure Island*. Along the way lies Bathurst Basin, originally one of three entrances into the Floating Harbour from the New Cut. Today, many small pleasure craft lie tied up in the Basin, overlooked by the attractive properties of Bathurst Parade and the Ostrich Inn.

The Ostrich Inn is a whitewashed, three-storey hostelry, with an inn sign depicting Bristol's great seafaring traditions. This theme continues inside the pub where ship's lamps, sturdy ropes, paintings of historic vessels and an assortment of old shipping documentation leave the visitor in no doubt as to the origins of the pub. At the far end of the bar is a diminutive caged cellar housing a skeleton, indicative of the fate that met stowaways or smugglers in centuries past.

The menu at the Ostrich is divided up into various sections that include fish dishes, meat dishes, pasta dishes and children's dishes. Lighter appetites might be attracted by the wide choice of baguettes and jacket potatoes, although it should be added that the menu describes the substantial baguettes as 'a meal in their own right'. Should your hunger still persist after a main course, the desserts include such tempting options as banoffi pie and chocolate fudge cake.

The beers available at the Ostrich include Theakston Old Peculier, Courage Best Bitter and John Smith's Bitter. If the elements permit, there can be few better places to enjoy a refreshing pint than seated at one of the picnic tables outside the Ostrich, overlooking Bathurst Basin. A truly evocative location in the heart of one of England's most historic ports.

Telephone: 0117 927 3774.

- **HOW TO GET THERE/PARKING:** Aim for the centre of Bristol, before following the signs for the SS *Great Britain*. This will

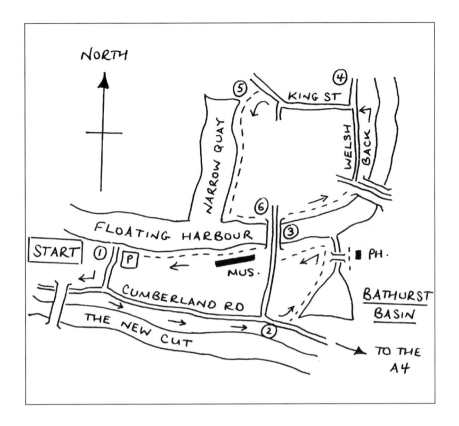

eventually take you along Cumberland Road to Gas Ferry Road, a cul-de-sac which leads down to the SS *Great Britain* car park (fee payable).

- **LENGTH OF THE WALK:** 3 miles. Maps: OS Landranger 172 Bristol and Bath or OS Explorer 154 Bristol West (GR 579723).

THE WALK

1. Follow Gas Ferry Road away from the SS *Great Britain* car park back up to Cumberland Road, and turn right to follow the main road alongside the New Cut. In 250 yards, there is a footbridge that crosses a railway line and the New Cut. Follow this footbridge across the railway, before following the steps on the right that descend to the path running between the tracks and the Cut itself. Having reached this path, turn left and follow the New Cut upstream for ³/₄ mile, latterly on the pavement beside Cumberland Road, until you reach a roundabout by the Louisiana pub.

2. Cross the road with care and follow the path alongside Bathurst Basin, the attractive waterside properties of Bathurst Parade to your left and the Ostrich Inn across the water on the right. There will be an opportunity to visit the inn later in the walk! When the path reaches the Floating Harbour, turn left and follow the path alongside Bathurst Wharf to Prince Street Swingbridge.

3. Cross the swingbridge and turn right just past Prince's Pantry to follow the opposite side of the Floating Harbour past the Mud Dock Café and the Thekla Floating Bar. Continue past the Thekla to the Hole in the Wall Restaurant and Redcliffe Way. Cross Redcliffe Way into the road opposite – Welsh Back – which runs alongside the Floating Harbour. A short distance along Welsh Back, turn right alongside the Children's Scrapstore to reach the quayside itself.

Follow the quayside for 200 yards towards Bristol Bridge, before turning left into King Street.

4. Continue along this historic cobbled street, passing the Llandogger Trow, the Old Duke and the Theatre Royal. At the far end of King Street, continue along Broad Quay for a few yards until you reach a pedestrian crossing by a statue of Brunel.

5. Cross the busy thoroughfare at this point, before heading down the nearside of Narrow Quay, the heart of the historic port of Bristol. At the far end of Narrow Quay, bear left past the Arnolfini Arts Centre to reach Prince Street and the swingbridge crossed earlier in the walk.

6. Cross the swingbridge, and take a detour to the left if you wish to visit the Ostrich Inn before completing the walk. To complete the actual walk, having crossed the swingbridge, turn right to follow Princes Wharf in front of Bristol's Industrial Museum. Continue following the quayside for ½ mile back to the SS *Great Britain* complex and the car park.

THE BRISTOL CHANNEL AT CLEVEDON

The sea, with its ebb and flow of tides, has long held a fascination and delight for everyone from the youngest to the oldest. This walk follows the coast path to the north of Clevedon, where clifftop vantage points bring expansive views towards the Welsh coast and the distant Welsh Hills.

Clevedon pier

The coastal resort of Clevedon sits somewhat sedately overlooking the Bristol Channel, on a rocky and pebbly stretch of coastline. The atmosphere is decidedly Victorian, with large grey limestone villas, public parks and bowling greens, although Georgian and Regency buildings tell of the town's gradual evolution from a fishing village to a small fashionable resort during the 19th century.

Dominating the seafront is Clevedon Pier, the town's most famous

Victorian landmark constructed in 1869 of iron rails originally intended for use on Brunel's South Wales Railway. During a safety check back in 1970, part of the pier's walkway collapsed, leaving the end pavilion standing forlornly at sea. For many years, the pier lay in a state of ruinous decay whilst frenetic fund-raising campaigns attempted to raise the cash needed for restoration work to commence. The campaign eventually bore fruit in the summer of 1998, when the pier was officially reopened to visitors. This would have pleased Sir John Betjeman, who wrote of Clevedon Pier: 'It recalls a painting by Turner, or an etching by Whistler or Sickert, or even a Japanese print ... Without its Pier, Clevedon would be a diamond with a flaw.' The walk follows the coast path to the north of the pier, which looks out onto the Bristol Channel, one of Britain's foremost shipping lanes. During the 17th and 18th centuries, Bristol was one of the world's greatest ports, and many a cargo of sugar, rum and tobacco from the West Indies would have sailed up through these waters. The Industrial Revolution saw the heyday of the South Wales Coalfield, with the ports at Cardiff and Barry becoming vast coal-exporting centres. During the 20th century the tables turned. Bulk cargoes of iron-ore and cheap imported coal now pour into the port installations at Port Talbot and Newport to supply the local steelworks, navigating a channel that has the second highest tidal range in the world. A rise and fall of tides of over 50 feet is not uncommon beneath the Severn Bridge.

Opposite the entrance to Clevedon Pier lies a bar and restaurant named Campbell's Landing. Campbell's paddle steamers used to navigate the Bristol Channel, visiting the resorts of Clevedon, Weston and Ilfracombe with their crowds of holidaymakers. The inn sign depicts a Campbell's vessel berthed at Clevedon, with crowds of Victorian holidaymakers thronging the pier.

Campbell's Landing attempts to recreate the atmosphere of the old steamers. The bar and restaurant are decorated with various items of Campbell's memorabilia – old timetables, publicity leaflets, historic photographs and a ship's figurehead. Even the toilets have a nautical feel, with their porthole windows and signs reading 'buoys' and 'gulls'. Arrive in good time, and you may be fortunate enough to find a window seat with views of the Channel itself.

The bar food consists of staple dishes such as soups, jacket potatoes and sandwiches, whilst there is also a varied restaurant menu. This contains selections grouped under headings such as

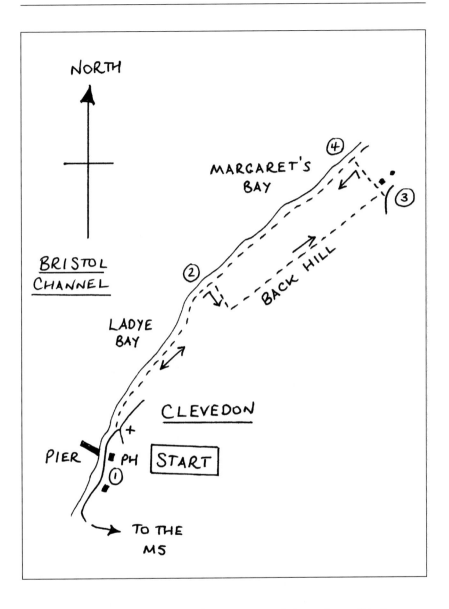

starters, fish dishes, grills and vegetarian dishes. Deep-fried cream cheese and Cumberland dip might appeal as a starter, perhaps followed by steak and kidney pie in stout. A number of beers are available at Campbell's Landing, including Ruddles, Courage Bitter, Beamish Stout and John Smith's. What could be better than

75

Campbell's Landing, Clevedon

appetising food and drink enjoyed in a bar overlooking the sea? Telephone: 01275 872094.

- **HOW TO GET THERE:** Leave the M5 motorway at junction 20, and follow the signs for Clevedon. On entering the town, follow the signs for the seafront, which will eventually take you to the town's pier.
- **PARKING:** There is free roadside parking on the seafront just below the pier.
- **LENGTH OF THE WALK:** 4 miles. Maps: OS Landranger 172 Bristol and Bath or OS Explorer 154 Bristol West (GR 402718).

THE WALK

1. Walk past the entrance to Clevedon Pier and on up Marine Parade for 250 yards to its junction with Wellington Terrace, alongside a large chapel. Turn left at this point along a coastal footpath – Lover's Walk – which is followed for $3/4$ mile through to Ladye Bay. Just before Ladye Bay, ignore a path going off on the right, and on reaching Ladye Bay, ignore the path sloping down on the left to the bay itself.

Continue instead for about 400 yards along the main coastal path as it climbs above Ladye Bay.

2. Turn right along an enclosed path that climbs steeply up from the coast onto Back Hill. In another 300 yards, at a junction on the hilltop, turn left and follow an enclosed path along the top of Back Hill alongside the local golf course. Follow this path for 1 mile, ignoring an early right turn, until the path drops downhill to a junction by a detached house.

3. Turn left at this point, cross a stile and follow the right edge of a field downhill to a stile and the coast path.

4. Turn left and follow the coast path for just over 1 mile back to Ladye Bay. Beyond Ladye Bay, retrace your steps along Lover's Walk and Marine Parade back to Clevedon's seafront and the pier.

THE BRISTOL CHANNEL AT SAND POINT AND MIDDLE HOPE

North of Weston-super-Mare, the limestone promontory of Middle Hope and Sand Point projects finger-like into the Bristol Channel. From the miniature cliffs that fall away to the sea there are fine views across the Channel towards the islands of Steep Holm and Flat Holm, and beyond to South Wales and the distant Brecon Beacons.

Middle Hope

Middle Hope and Sand Point form a limestone peninsula, steeped in history, at the northern end of Sand Bay. Across the flat hilltop, there are traces of banks thought to represent early prehistoric field-systems. Archaeological excavations have revealed two Iron Age settlements, Romano-British pottery fragments and a 4th-century coin of the Valentinian period.

Castle Batch is a Norman motte, whose mound and ditch were

unfortunately disturbed during wartime construction work at the site. At one time, Sand Point and Middle Hope probably formed an island, only accessible at low tide across the surrounding mudflats. This would have made it a fine site for defensive settlement, and would explain its long history of human habitation.

Many years ago, lead mining took place on Middle Hope, and several of the tracks hereabouts represent the courses of old tramways. Mining shafts have been discovered over the years, and one such 'secret tunnel' uncovered by Boy Scouts in the 1930s was immediately filled in for safety reasons.

The area was also the scene of the 'Secret War' during the 1939–45 hostilities. Unusual experiments took place on Middle Hope that involved a pair of high speed catapult tracks laid down for missile testing. These missiles were said to be 'unlike any seen in the history of modern warfare'.

At the end of the walk, a 1 mile drive south along the coast road – or a gentle stroll across the foreshore of Sand Bay – will bring you to the Long John Silver pub. This whitewashed Wadworth inn faces Sand Bay, with the tables at the front of the hostelry being an ideal place to enjoy refreshment on a fine day. Internally, the Long John Silver maintains a decidedly nautical theme. Fishing nets, lifebuoys, ships' wheels and photographs of old sailing vessels decorate the main bar area, along with a fine oil painting of the infamous character from the Treasure Island novel. Lovers of the sea will also spot a case of knots, a display of cigarette cards with a nautical theme and a navigation chart of the Bristol Channel.

A range of bar food is offered to customers at the Long John Silver, with selections including plaice, cod, lasagne, chicken Kiev, chicken nuggets and beefburgers. Filled rolls and toasted sandwiches are also available to satisfy lighter appetites. To accompany your meal, Wadworth 6X would seem a natural choice. There are a number of other fine real ales available, however, including Badger Best Bitter and Adnams Bitter.

Telephone: 01934 623367.

● **HOW TO GET THERE/PARKING:** From Weston-super-Mare's seafront, follow the signs to Sand Bay. Beyond Birnbeck Pier, this involves a section of toll-road that skirts Worlebury Hill. The road northwards through Sand Bay passes the Long John Silver before ending at Middle Hope, where there is a large NT car park.

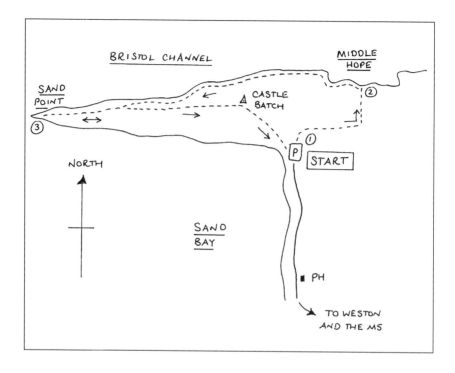

● **LENGTH OF THE WALK:** 2½ miles. Maps: OS Landranger 182 Weston and Bridgwater or OS Explorer 153 Weston-super-Mare (GR 320659).

THE WALK

1. Leave the car park and turn right. At the entrance to Middle Hope, there are two options. Ignore the steps on the left, rather follow the unmetalled track that bears right. In 50 yards, turn left up a stepped path signposted 'To the Headland'. At the top of these steps, cross a stile and turn right, following a fence on the right that forms the boundary of the hilltop enclosure. Along the way, you will pass a ruinous stone wall on the left, and enjoy fine views on the right across the low-lying farmland bordering the Channel. In the corner of this field, turn left and follow a stone wall down to the coast itself.

2. On reaching the shoreline, turn left and follow the edge of the field westwards, literally clinging as close as possible to the

80

Standing at the trig point on Middle Hope

coastline. Initially the path borders a pebble-strewn bay before following the tops of some low-lying cliffs. Follow this path as it runs below the ridge that crosses Middle Hope. In ³/₄ mile, where the field ends, continue along the path beyond a gateway that climbs uphill towards the ridge. Continue along this path to Sand Point, at the far western end of Middle Hope.

3. Having paused to enjoy the views across the Bristol Channel towards Wales, retrace your steps back along the ridge heading towards the car park. Ignore the path that bears left down to the cliff edge – followed earlier on the walk – keeping instead to the higher ridge-top path. In 600 yards, the path reaches Castle Batch and the trig point on Middle Hope. Continue past the trig point, following the path that bears right downhill back to the car park.

On reaching the car park, it is a few minutes' drive along the coast road to the Long John Silver. Alternatively, why not enjoy a stroll across the foreshore of Sandy Bay to the inn? The walk back to the car park will then burn off any calories taken on board!

AROUND BLAGDON LAKE

Enjoy a walk in and around the fringes of Blagdon Lake, in the heart of Bristol's very own 'Lake District'. Tucked in beneath the northern slopes of the Mendip Hills, Blagdon's reputation for wildfowl and trout attracts ornithologists and fly-fishermen from far and wide.

Blagdon Lake

Blagdon Lake is one of Bristol's main reservoirs, formed by damming the river Yeo way back in 1901. This vast stretch of open water – 1½ miles in length and ½ mile wide – covers an area of some 430 acres. It is rich in wildfowl – including widgeon, teal and pochard in the winter months and great crested grebe and ruddy duck in the summer – which does mean that a pair of binoculars are almost obligatory on this particular waterside walk.

Blagdon Lake is also renowned for its quite excellent fly-fishing, with anglers dotted around the lakeside and offshore on their rowing boats seeking to capture that often elusive brown or rainbow trout. The start of the fly-fishing season is so eagerly anticipated at Blagdon that some anglers camp out for as long as 48 hours in their vehicles to secure the best pitches.

Although it is not possible to literally walk along the side of Blagdon Lake for more than perhaps a couple of miles on this walk, the fieldpaths, lanes and byways are never more than a few hundred yards from the water's edge. As you enjoy a slight elevation for much of the circuit, the views across the water are quite excellent, especially from the lanes that run along the hillside to the north of Blagdon. From this side of the water, the true splendour of Blagdon Lake, set against a backdrop of the Mendip Hills, can be fully appreciated.

Above the lake lies the village of Blagdon, dominated by its majestic 15th-century church whose 116 foot high Somerset tower is a landmark visible from all over the district. Other than the 15th-century tower, St Andrew's was largely rebuilt in 1909 by Lord Winterstoke, a member of the Wills family, Bristol's tobacco barons. The most celebrated incumbent of the church was the Reverend Augustus Toplady, who held the living between 1762 and 1764. Toplady is best known for writing the hymn *Rock of Ages*, inspired whilst sheltering from a thunderstorm in nearby Burrington Combe.

A little way down Church Street from St Andrew's stands the New Inn, ironically the oldest inn in the village! This cottage-style hostelry, whose rear garden enjoys spectacular views across Blagdon Lake, dates back to the 16th century when it served as a cider house. Internally, the New Inn is made up of two very traditional bar areas, decorated with ancient beams, horse brasses and a collection of tankards. Antique settles and comfortable armchairs will offer welcome respite after this fairly lengthy excursion deep in North Somerset, with log fires in inglenook fireplaces adding warmth in winter months.

In addition to soup, sandwiches and ploughman's, the New Inn offers such tempting dishes as filled Yorkshire puddings, home-made steak and kidney pie, lasagne, vegetable chilli and steaks, as well as a tempting range of desserts. Being a Wadworth inn, such fine beers as 6X and Henry's IPA are available, although many visitors may enjoy a pint of Butcombe Bitter, brewed locally in a small village just across the lake from the New Inn.

Telephone: 01761 462475.

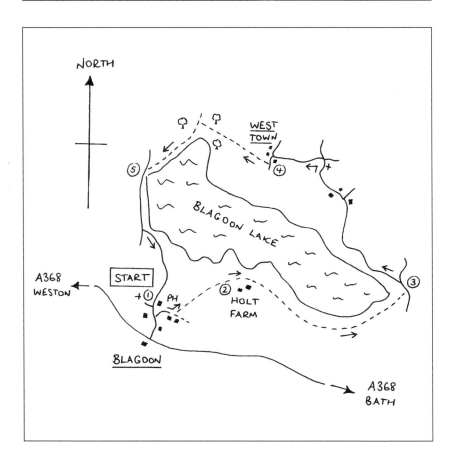

- **HOW TO GET THERE:** Blagdon lies on the A368 Bath to Weston-super-Mare road, 4 miles east of its junction with the A38 at Churchill. Turn off the main road opposite the Ring o' Bells pub into Church Street. The New Inn lies 250 yards down Church Street, just past the cul-de-sac lane leading to St Andrew's church.
- **PARKING:** There is a car park for patrons at the New Inn. There is also room for careful roadside parking in Church Street near the inn, including a couple of spaces outside St Andrew's church.
- **LENGTH OF THE WALK:** 6 miles. Maps: OS Landranger 172 Bristol and Bath or OS Explorer 4 Mendip Hills West and 154 Bristol West (GR 505590).

The New Inn, Blagdon

THE WALK

1. Walk back up Church Street for 100 yards towards the A368 before turning left into Grib Lane, a quiet cul-de-sac. Where Grib Lane ends, continue along a grassy path in front of a pair of houses on the right. Immediately past the last house, cross a stile on the left and follow a short section of enclosed path to a second stile and an open field, overlooking Blagdon Lake. Follow the right edge of this field to its bottom corner, cross a pair of stiles on the right following a path that clips the corner of a small area of scrub and join an unmetalled farm track. Follow this track to the right towards Holt Farm.

In 150 yards, halfway to Holt Farm, cross a stile on the left into an adjoining field. Bear right, and head across this field aiming for the left edge of the complex of buildings that form Holt Farm.

2. Cross two stiles to the left of the farm buildings before following the right edge of the field beyond the farm. In the far corner of this field, just by Holt Copse, cross a pair of stiles on the right-hand side. Continue walking in the same direction as before, this time with the hedgerow on the left. For the next mile, keep walking in the same

85

direction, a hedge on your left, crossing several fields and passing through a number of spinneys, until you join a lane at the eastern end of Blagdon Lake. Throughout this section of the walk, the lake is just beyond the hedgerow on the left.

3. Turn left along the lane and, in just 75 yards, left at a junction to follow the turning signposted to Nempnett and Butcombe. In $3/4$ mile, ignore the right turn – aptly named Awkward Hill – and continue along the lane that you have been following all the while – Chapel Lane. In another $1/4$ mile, at a minor crossroads by an old chapel, turn left. In 600 yards, where this lane bears right by Bellevue Farm, turn left along a cul-de-sac signposted 'No access to the lake'.

4. In just 25 yards, cross a stone slab stile on the right and follow a fieldpath directly across four fields, visible stiles marking the course of the right-of-way.

At the far side of the fourth field, follow a woodland path for 200 yards to a footbridge over a stream. Cross the stile at the far end of the bridge, turn left and follow the edge of the field to a stile in the corner and a second footbridge. At the far side of this bridge, cross the stile on the left and continue along the path that now borders Blagdon Lake. Follow this lakeside path for $1/2$ mile, crossing one further footbridge along the way.

5. Cross a stile to join a lane on the northern edge of the dam that was constructed to form Blagdon Lake. Follow the lane to the left, crossing the dam, all the while enjoying the views that extend the whole length of the lake. At the far side of the dam, turn left and follow Park Lane for $1/2$ mile back up into Blagdon village, where the lane emerges by the New Inn and St Andrew's church. Ignore one right turn – Dark Lane – along the way.

PLACES OF INTEREST NEARBY

Just a mile-or-two south of Blagdon lies the village of *Burrington Combe*. It was whilst sheltering in a cleft in the rock face at this Mendip settlement that the Reverend Augustus Toplady was inspired to write the hymn *Rock of Ages*. The world famous cleft is now a popular tourist attraction.

CHEW VALLEY LAKE

Just a few miles south of Bristol lies the Chew Valley, bounded to the north by Dundry Hill and to the south by the Mendips. In the heart of the valley lies Chew Valley Lake, a vast reservoir with 10 miles of shoreline. This walk includes a stretch of lakeside path, followed by a stroll along the river Chew.

The river Chew

Modern society has a virtually insatiable appetite for water. It was for this reason that the Bristol Waterworks Company had always cast an envious eye over the supply potential of the Chew Valley. Geological surveys in 1934 confirmed their beliefs, but the onset of the Second World War temporarily thwarted plans for reservoir development. Construction of the reservoir commenced, however, in 1950 with a 500 yard long dam creating an artificial lake that was 2½ miles long, and possessed a capacity of some 4,500 million gallons. The Queen performed the opening ceremony in 1956.

As well as supplying water, the reservoir is an important leisure amenity. Fishermen travel considerable distances to fish for the scientifically stocked brown and rainbow trout, with Chew having a reputation as perhaps the finest lake for trout fishing in Europe. For the ornithologist it is an important centre for winter wildfowl, with diving birds like the pochard and the tufted duck being especially common.

The walk itself begins in the nearby village of Chew Magna, described by Leland, Henry VIII's antiquary, as a 'praty cloathing toun'. The fine Georgian houses alongside the raised pavements tell of Chew's later prosperity when it became home to many of Bristol's more affluent business and professional people. To this day it remains a large commuter village, unspoiled by modern development due to its Conservation Area status. St Andrew's church dates from the 15th century, and as well as possessing a tower almost 100 feet in height, it contains an uncommon wooden effigy, a knight, allegedly Sir John de Hauteville.

Having explored the countryside south of the village, the walk returns to Chew Magna by way of Chew Valley Lake and the river Chew. At journey's end lies the Pelican Inn. A story is told of a pelican that once escaped wing-clipping time at Bristol Zoo and flew south to discover Chew Valley Lake. After a few days' vacation in what must have seemed like pelican heaven, the intrepid bird was recaptured and returned to face his delayed encounter with the clippers!

This whitewashed hostelry is part of the Ushers empire, the West Country brewery based in Trowbridge. The inn fronts onto Chew Magna's High Street, and is a picture in the summer months with its tubs and hanging baskets full of colourful floral displays. Inside the Pelican are a comfortably furnished lounge and public bar, with exposed stonework, wooden wall panelling and black beams creating a traditional atmosphere. There is, as befits a country pub, a stone fireplace, whilst around the walls are displayed a number of rustic prints.

A good range of traditional pub food is available at the Pelican. Lighter appetites might fancy a salad or a ploughman's, whilst heartier appetites will be drawn to dishes such as steak and kidney pie, chicken and mushroom pie, lasagne or curry. Ushers beers are, of course, on offer here, including Founders, Best Bitter and Triple Crown. After this delightful waterside excursion in the Chew Valley,

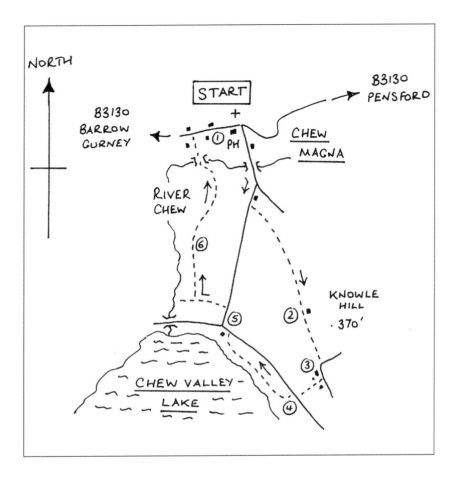

a refreshing pint in the inn's garden will complete a perfect day in the countryside.
Telephone: 01275 332448.

- **HOW TO GET THERE:** Chew Magna lies south of Bristol on the B3130, the road that links the A37 at Pensford with the A38 at Barrow Gurney.
- **PARKING:** There is a public car park in the centre of Chew Magna behind the Pelican Inn. The car park is signposted in the middle of the village.
- **LENGTH OF THE WALK:** 4 miles. Maps: OS Landranger 172 Bristol and Bath or OS Explorer 154 Bristol West (GR 576632).

Chew Valley Lake

THE WALK

1. Leave the car park and turn right in front of the Pelican Inn before taking the first turning on the right signposted to Bishop Sutton and Bath. Follow this road – Moorledge Road – for 600 yards, crossing the river Chew and passing the local fire station, before turning right along Denny Lane. In 150 yards, turn left along an enclosed footpath, shown on the OS sheets as Pitt's Lane. Continue along this enclosed path for just under ½ mile until you enter an open field. Continue along the left edge of this field until you reach Pitt's Farm, whose collection of buildings have now been converted for residential use.

2. The path bears right in front of a modernised farm cottage to a clearly visible stile. Once across this stile, follow the left-hand field boundary to a stile halfway along the left edge of the field. Continue along an enclosed path, a residential property on the left, until you reach a handgate and the common land surrounding Knowle Hill. Continue directly ahead along the right edge of the common land, Knowle Hill to the left. Keep on this path as it enters a patch of woodland, before descending to join a lane by Knowle Hill Farm.

3. Turn right along the lane and pass in front of Knowle House before turning right along a signposted footpath that follows the gravelled driveway down to the Old Granary. It does seem rather like entering private residential property, but remember these were just old farm buildings until recent conversion to domestic use. Pass in front of the Old Granary before crossing a gate on the left into an open field. Turn right, and follow the right edge of the field to a stile in the bottom corner. Follow the right edge of the next field to a gate in the corner where you join the Bishop Sutton to Chew Stoke road.

4. Turn right along this road for a few yards, before turning left into a picnic area by Chew Valley Lake. Pass through a small copse to the parking area, and turn right. Follow the path across a picnic area, beyond which it becomes enclosed and literally follows the side of the lake. Continue along this lakeside path for 1/2 mile to a second picnic area, before turning right out of the car park to rejoin the Chew Stoke road.

5. Turn left along the road for a few yards, before turning right along Denny Lane. In just 150 yards, turn left along a waterboard access road which is signposted as a footpath. Follow this road downhill until, just before a bridge across the river Chew, you turn right along a signposted path into an area of woodland. Follow the woodland path to a stile, before continuing through another area of woodland to a second stile and open fields.

6. Head directly across the next five fields, following the river Chew upstream for close on 1 mile, stiles marking the course of the right-of-way. The river meanders across the meadows, with the right-of-way following a more direct route just to the right of the water's edge. At the far side of the fifth field, cross a stile and follow a short section of enclosed path to the right to a junction. Turn left and follow a path across a small stream and onto a second footbridge, this bridge crossing the Chew. Once across the river, turn right and follow a path uphill for 150 yards to reach the B3130 in Chew Magna. Turn right to return to the centre of the village and the Pelican Inn.

THE RESERVOIRS AT LITTON

✦❧✦

The Eastern Mendips are characterised by gentle hills and lush valleys, a vivid contrast with the more rugged landscape of limestone cliffs and crags found in West Mendip. Deep in a fold in the hills at Litton lie of pair of diminutive reservoirs, the home of a rich variety of wildfowl.

Litton Reservoir

The reservoirs at Litton were constructed by Irish navvies in the mid-19th century. The lower reservoir was completed in 1846, followed by the upper reservoir just four years later. At the time, Catholicism was not widely practised in this corner of Somerset, and the migrant labourers caused something of a stir when mass was said in Litton church. There are also accounts of these navvies kneeling in the mud around the mill at Sherborne Farm in Litton whilst practising their faith.

These stretches of water were constructed as 'compensation

reservoirs' by the damming of the river Chew. The source of the Chew is found at a number of springs a mile or so upstream near the village of Chewton Mendip, springs that the Bristol Waterworks Company used for its water supplies. The reservoirs were used to prevent local residents from having their supplies disrupted when the springs were being drawn upon for supply purposes.

The peaceful waters of Litton's reservoirs are home to a variety of wildfowl including coot, moorhen, swan, mallard and tufted duck. The habitats around the lakeside are also home to a range of flora and fauna that includes foxes and badgers, reed warblers and pied wagtails and peacock and tortoiseshell butterflies, a veritable naturalist's paradise. A final element of interest on the water is the section of reservoir below the upper dam that is cordoned off with a net. This area is used by the water company to rear fish, and not surprisingly it acts as a magnet for the local wildfowl.

Before exploring the Litton Reservoirs, however, the walk follows quiet byways and lanes across the undulating countryside south of Litton. Stoneyard Lane, whose verges are awash with traditional English flora in springtime, gives the walk a gentle elevation that brings fine views northwards across that fold in the hills that hides the Litton Reservoirs. Along the way, the walk also passes close to Eastwood Manor Farm, where dairy cattle were traditionally stalled in a remarkable Victorian steading. That dramatic building across the fields that resembles Joseph Paxton's burnt Crystal Palace was designed in 1858 by Robert Smith, agent of John and Frederic Knight.

Back in Litton at journey's end, appetites and thirsts can be satisfied at the King's Arms. This 15th-century whitewashed hostelry, reached by descending a flight of steps from the car park, exudes a real sense of history. Polished flagstones, heavy beams, a vast fireplace, settles and wheelback chairs give a real feeling of having stepped back in time. There is even a suit of armour in an alcove in one of the bar areas.

In addition to sandwiches and salads, an extensive selection of dishes is available at the King's Arms. These might typically include lamb cutlets, king prawns in garlic butter, chicken and broccoli bake and marinated pork ribs with sour cream and barbecue sauce. A good range of beers is served at this fine old inn, including Bass, Courage Best and Wadworth 6X. If the weather is favourable, refreshment can be enjoyed at one of the many picnic tables in the

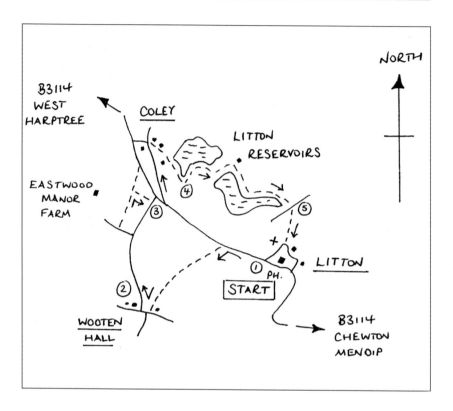

tiered gardens, which slope attractively down to the river Chew.
Telephone: 01761 241301.

- **HOW TO GET THERE:** Litton lies on the B3114 between Chewton
  Mendip (A39) and West Harptree (A368). As you drive through the
  village, the King's Arms lies alongside the main road.
- **PARKING:** There is a large car park for patrons by the King's Arms.
  Walkers may prefer to park in the village initially. Driving through
  Litton from Chewton Mendip, turn right just past the King's Arms
  onto a quiet lane that leads into the centre of the village. Follow
  this lane around to the village hall, where there is room for careful
  roadside parking. Alternatively, again entering from Chewton
  Mendip, you could park in the layby by the telephone box.
- **LENGTH OF THE WALK:** 3^1/$_2$ miles. Maps: OS Landranger 182
  Weston-super-Mare and Bridgwater or OS Explorer 4 Mendip Hills
  West (GR 594546).

The 15th-century pub at the start of the walk

THE WALK

1. Turn right outside the King's Arms and follow the B3114 westwards for ¼ mile with care – there is no pavement. Turn left after ¼ mile onto a signposted byway, shown on the OS sheets as Stoneyard Lane. Follow Stoneyard Lane gently uphill for ½ mile to a quiet lane in the hamlet of Wooten Hall, with the lane becoming an unmetalled path for the last 300 yards of its length. Turn right at the road and, at a junction in just 30 yards, keep on this road as it bears to the right.

2. Continue downhill for 600 yards to a road junction, enjoying fine views to the north towards Coley Hill. Turn left at this junction and, in 150 yards, cross a stile on the right to follow a signposted footpath that runs downhill along the right edge of two fields. Away to the left stand the unusual buildings of Eastwood Manor Farm. Just before the bottom corner of the second field, cross a gate on the right and follow the hedge on the right across to the far corner of the adjoining field. Cross a stile and descend some steps to a lane, before turning left to reach the B3114.

3. Turn right and, in just a few yards, left down a slip road which is followed for 600 yards into Coley. Just past a junction as you enter the village, turn right along a farm track by a bungalow, signposted as a footpath. Follow this track for 250 yards, passing an assortment of farm buildings, until you reach a waterboard installation on the right. Continue past this building to a cattle grid. Rather than crossing the cattle grid to reach the dam at the end of Litton's lower reservoir, pass through the gateway directly ahead. Follow the hedge on the left across two fields to a footbridge across a stream in the far right-hand corner of the second field.

4. Cross this footbridge, and turn left to follow this woodland stream down to Litton Reservoirs. Continue following the path along the water's edge to the dam between the two reservoirs. Cross the dam, turn right in front of the cottage on the far side and follow the northern bank of the upper reservoir for ½ mile to its eastern end. Just before crossing the footbridge at this far end of the reservoir, turn left through a gap in the hedgerow to reach Whitehouse Lane.

5. Cross a stile opposite, and follow the right edge of the next three fields alongside the river Chew to a gate in the far right-hand corner of the third field. Leave the field and join the lane in the centre of Litton. Turn right, cross the Chew and continue along the lane as it bears left to return to the B3114. A left turn brings you back to the King's Arms.

PLACES OF INTEREST NEARBY

The nearest towns to Litton are *Midsomer Norton* and *Radstock*, at one time the centre of the coal-mining industry in North Somerset. The local museum offers visitors an insight into the unique history of the local mining communities – and includes a replica coal-face (telephone 01761 437722). At nearby Chewton Mendip lies the *Chewton Cheese Dairy*, where visitors can observe different aspects of cheese making each day, as well as enjoying the opportunity to sample some quite excellent Cheddar (telephone 01761 241666).